Ex Libris

Elder

The Conversion of the Irish

From St. Patrick to 700 AD

A Study of the Relationship between Gospel and Culture

The Rev. Lawrence D. Bausch
Holy Trinity Parish
San Diego, California

© 2007

ISBN EAN 9780967763583

Ekklesia Society Publications
PO Box 118526
Carrollton, TX 75011-8526
www.ekk.org

Contents

Acknowledgements

My summer sabbatical study in Ireland and the subsequent opportunity to complete my study and put it into this book has been possible through the generosity and support of many people, at least a few of whom I would like to thank here.

First of all, I thank my wife, Carol, my four children, Adam, Eric, Evan and Laurel, and my mother and stepfather, Irma and Jack Howard (both since deceased), whose love, encouragement and support throughout the entire process from Anniversary to Sabbatical enabled me to first dream of this project, and then fulfill the dream.

Second, I thank the people of Holy Trinity Parish in Ocean Beach, California, who enabled me to take sabbatical leave in commemoration with a celebration of my 25th Anniversary as a priest, held in January 2001. In particular, I thank three members who encouraged and coordinated this effort: Susan Batt, Lori Changala, and Laury Graves. My special thanks also goes out to John Jenkins, whose purchase of seemingly endless boxes of cereals and crackers brought much food to our Food Bank and many frequent flyer miles to me.

Third, I thank The Rev. Frank Maguire, native of Ireland, who helped provide me with good questions which helped to focus my study, and also with people in Ireland who gave further guidance.

In Ireland, I received indispensable guidance from three priests, Fr. Brian Macraois and Fr. Neil Carlin, both Roman Catholics, and Fr. Peter Barrett, Anglican.

During my three months away, I was able to entrust the care of Holy Trinity to Fr. Boone Sadler (now deceased) and Fr. Victor Krulak, plus Parish Administrator Marian Smith. Between their work and the Vestry and people of Holy Trinity, I was free from worry throughout the entire summer I was in Ireland.

I am also grateful to several people who helped me to continue my writing following my return. Both Roger Hovey and his wife, Lori Changala, and John and Teresa Hardisty, provided me quiet places to reflect and write. Also, Fr. Maguire, Susan Batt, Sandra Mack and Emily Evans provided helpful critiques during various revisions, with Susan and Sandra also providing technical support.

I owe a debt of gratitude to Canon Bill Atwood of Ekklesia for his willingness to publish my work.

Finally, I extend profound thanks to St. Patrick, whose intercession and example have inspired and challenged me for more than 30 years. Like him, I am not Irish, but, like him, I too found in Ireland a place where the living Presence of the Holy Trinity is especially manifest.

Introduction

For more than 1,000 years, Western Europe has been predominantly Christian, with Biblical underpinnings to most of its political and cultural values. Similarly, since their beginnings, the countries of North America have been "Judeo-Christian" as well. As a consequence, those of us who inhabit historical churches and profess Christian faith do so in the context of an historically supportive culture. However, since the second half of the twentieth century, both Western Europe and North America have seen the dramatic rise of a cultural pluralism that has been increasingly successful in removing Christianity from its special place at the center of the dominant culture. These countries have determined to take a position of religious neutrality, from which all belief systems are to be treated with equal respect, while none may be permitted to dominate our national lives. This official neutrality on the part of Western leaders was reflected recently when the heir to the British crown, Prince Charles, while a churchgoing Anglican, proclaimed his intention, upon becoming King, to be known as "Defender of faith" rather than the traditional "Defender of the Faith," with its obvious Christian implications. Against this backdrop, Christians in the West are having to rethink our place in our culture, and are challenged to examine the relationship between Gospel and culture in ways not heretofore necessary. How do we distinguish the changeless Gospel and the divinely instituted organism which is the Body of Christ, the Church, from the cultural accretions within which Western Christians have lived for centuries and which, in the emerging post-Christian culture, may have to change?

It is in the light of this urgent evangelical and missionary question that this study will examine the process of the conversion of the Irish from a pagan people to Christianity. This segment of Christian history is particularly relevant in this regard for several reasons. First, it is the best-documented effort to spread the Gospel beyond the Roman Empire. It provides a rare opportunity to see how the Gospel, which came into the world in the middle of the Empire's 1,000-year dominance and spread largely within it, took root in a different culture. Second, during the roughly 250 years between the arrival of the first missionary bishop and the virtually complete Christianizing of the Irish, there are no records of any martyrs. This phenomenon alone makes this episode in Christian missions unique.[1] Moreover, it underscores the success of the mission. Third, while the orthodox, conciliar Christian faith was received fully in Ireland, with no significant evidence of the major heresies after the time of Patrick, the structures of the Church found throughout the Empire were greatly changed. In studying this, we can see which components of the Church were regarded as essential to be faithful to Christ's intention, and which components were regarded as of limited value and subject to change in a different culture.

The intention in this work is to explore the ways in which the Gospel was communicated during the period of the conversion of the Irish. How did Christians evangelize? Can we see in their means of sharing the faith some reasons for their success? We will begin in

---

[1] There is evidence that this was also the case in Mexico, but there the Gospel came with political and military strength.

Chapter One with a survey of some elements of Irish life in the fifth century, learning something about the people to whom the Gospel would be presented. Chapter Two will explore the mission of St. Patrick, so well presented in his two extant writings. In Chapter Three we will examine the establishment of the Christian Church in the two centuries following Patrick, which reveals the radical change in Church organization from that found in the Empire, and also the evangelical impetus for such changes. Chapter Four will illustrate how the Gospel was communicated in representative writings from the monastic communities of the sixth and seventh centuries. In the conclusion, we will re-examine some key elements of the Irish experience, looking at some ways in which what took place then and there can assist us as we face the challenge of mission in our changing culture.

In writing this study, I am making no claims as a scholar of Irish history. I spent the summer of 2001 on sabbatical in Ireland, and was able to see about 75% of the best-preserved early Christian sites. After a glorious visit to Skellig Michael, I ran into Des Lavalle at the Skellig Experience on Valentia Island. In a copy of his book "The Skellig Story" which I purchased, he wrote, "One visit is not enough." That is certainly true, and not only of Skellig Michael! Also, my reading of the primary sources for this study is severely limited by my lack of language skills. As a result, I have only been able to read what is available in translation. Moreover, I am a parish priest, and my approach to this topic is more pastoral and evangelical than scholarly. Nevertheless, I hope to honor the ancient documents and their authors enough to let them speak for themselves. I wholly accept the historian's responsibility described by Jean Mabillon and quoted by Thomas O'Loughlin in his important book, Celtic

Theology: "If he is honest...he must present as certain things certain; as false, things false; and as doubtful, things doubtful; he must not seek to hide facts that tell for or against either party to our issue. Piety and truth must not ever be considered as separable, for honest and genuine piety will never come into conflict with truth."[2]

---

[2] Celtic Theology, T. O'Loughlin, pp 6-7 [sp. Mabillon]

Chapter One

Aspects of Religious Society in Pre-Christian Ireland

The Celts had been in Ireland for perhaps 1,000 years before the arrival of Patrick in the fifth century A.D. Over that span of time, their culture had become established throughout the land. This was accomplished without the benefit of towns, cultural or educational centers, or a written language. Their spoken Celtic language had come to prevail also, as had certain religious beliefs and practices, social structure, and a body of law. However, our knowledge of pagan Ireland is quite limited. "In the absence of writings by Irish non-Christians themselves, we have these possible sources of information: archaeology, what Roman non-Christians wrote about the religion of the Celts (usually in Gaul several centuries earlier), and what later Christians wrote about their pagan ancestors. All these sources are limited, and even together they tell us very little."[3] We can hope, however, to highlight a few basic elements.

Underneath the few details we can observe of pagan Irish beliefs is perhaps the most important conviction: their high view of creation. For them, observable nature was soaked in the supernatural, and the portals between this world and the otherworld were everywhere. Nature, for the Irish Celts, was not a closed system. "...It is...as if the pagan Irish lived and breathed with one foot in this world and one foot in the otherworld; the two worlds

---

[3] St. Patrick: The Man & His Works, Thomas O'Loughlin, p 32

interpenetrated."[4] As a rural people, their dependence upon nature was complete, and, with this sense that all natural things were subject to supernatural influence, these people had a profound mixture of fear and reverence in relationship to all created things.

Many natural phenomena were identified as especially sacred, and it is likely that for the Irish, as for most pagans, the sun was singled out for special reverence. In most cases, this view reflects the awareness of the dependence that all life has upon it. Although we have little specific evidence of sun worship in Ireland, we do find Patrick making mention of it in his *Confession.* Contrasting the authority of the sun with that of Christ, he wrote, "For the sun is that which we see rising daily at His command, but it will never reign, nor will its splendour last forever. And all those who worship it will be subject to grievous punishment. We, however, worship the true sun, Christ, who will never perish. Nor will those who do His bidding, but they will continue forever just as Christ will continue forever, He Who reigns with God the Father Almighty and with the Holy Spirit before time and now and in eternity. Amen."[5]

In addition to the sun, some natural phenomena were regarded as places where divinities either dwelt or made their entrance into our world. Given the importance of water to a rural people, it is not surprising that rivers and wells were so regarded, often associated with "fertility and motherhood and also with strength, destruction and purification."[6] Wells in particular were revered as entrances to the otherworld, the timeless realm beyond this world.

---

[4] St. Patrick's World, Liam de Paor, p 29
[5] St. Patrick's World, p 108 (C60)
[6] A History of the Irish Church 400-700 A.D., John Walsh & Thomas Bradley, p 30

Similarly, certain trees and groves were especially revered. While the particulars of why oaks, yews, hazels and rowans should have been singled out may be opaque to us, one can see why in general trees were so regarded. In their very structure, they provide a link to all these dimensions – the roots, reaching down into the underworld; the visible portions in the world; and the growing ever upwards, reaching towards the heavens. Additionally, "they are not inanimate but living and so could be seen as being possessed by a god or spirit; leafless in winter but covered in foliage in summer, they represent fertility and rebirth; they have a certain indestructibility and resistance to the elements of fire and water."[7]

In the animal world, certain creatures were also especially revered. Birds were seen as "otherworldly agents, emblems of the gods, heralds of death, and portents of good or bad fortune."[8] We gain an insight into how common this belief was in reading from the Lorica attributed to Colum Cille (Columba), "I do not adore the voices of birds...My Druid is Christ the Son of God."[9] Certain other animals were also believed to be mediums of various divinities, including the horse, stag and boar among others. Indeed, it may be said that anything and everything in the world had the potential to be a vehicle for the gods of the pagan Irish.

As to the pantheon of Irish divinities, what we do know suggests that there was less specialization than that found in either Rome or Gaul. In an overview of the Irish pantheon, the late scholar Liam de Paor provides a helpful summary: "Goddesses appear in every part of Ireland as spirits of place – whole territories, or hilltops, rivers and springs – and as divinities of natural forces of motherhood,

---

[7] Walsh & Bradley, p 31
[8] Walsh & Bradley, p 34
[9] Walsh & Bradley, p 34

fertility, growth and destruction. They were often triple in character. War goddesses, in the form of crows or ravens, presided over the battlefield. The male divinities were warriors, craftsmen, magicians, seers, and nurturers, with, in crucial figures such as the Dagda (the 'good god'), an emphasis on feasting and consumption generally. But there is little evidence for any central organizing principle in the complexity of the pantheon…"[10]

In this world, for the pagan Irish everything that existed, everything that happened, was fraught with meaning that went beyond the merely natural. As such, life in this world was understood to be dangerous, demanding an ever-increasing sensitivity to the signs that were lurking everywhere. This gave rise to what we would call superstitions. Any behaviors that could be believed to give one a bit of safety and security in this world would be readily embraced. "Most of what we can guess about pre-Christian Ireland suggests a tissue of magical practices and rituals, the observance of omens, the use of spells and incantatory formulas and the avoidance of unlucky actions."[11] This religious outlook is both reflected in and is a reflection of Irish society at that time, and it is to that which we shall now turn.

As we noted earlier, Ireland in the fourth and fifth centuries boasted no towns. Rather, it was characterized by rural tribes or kingdoms. During this period, it has been estimated that there were between eighty and one hundred-fifty such communities. What united the people of Ireland were a common language, common beliefs and manner of living, and a certain social structure. Their religious beliefs were not peripheral to life but central, and this was

---

[10] St. Patrick's World, p 29
[11] St. Patrick's World, p 29

reflected in social organization. As Liam de Paor points out, "There are clear indications of a deep-rooted tradition in which the local 'king' was a sacral person, controlled by grievous taboos, acting as a kind of lightning-conductor to protect a pastoral and agricultural people against the arbitrary forces of nature, such as drought, storm, famine, lightning and disease, imagined as malevolent interventions by divinities or otherworld beings. The king was bound to the land and territory of his people and, in a common pattern, was the mate of the goddess of place who confirmed sovereignty on him."[12] This provision shows the extent to which the religious beliefs of the people overshadowed everything else. Even their tribal leaders were subservient to the gods.

Within the kingdoms, there were several classes of religious functionaries, such as the Druids referred to in the quote from Colum Cille, who expressed and maintained the culture. Again, from Professor de Paor: "We have reasonably abundant (although late) evidence for the presence in Ireland of special classes of sacral people corresponding to the bards, *vates* and druids described in Continental and British Celtic societies. The *filid*, or poets, were men of learning and long training and were possessed of supernatural powers. The *fáith*, corresponding to the vates, appears to have been a kind of soothsayer, while the *druí* (druid) had access to arcane knowledge and seems, in common belief, to have had some control over both natural and extra-natural powers. They formed a part of the retinue of the sacral king, and should probably be regarded as the repository of all tribal wisdom and knowledge. Their order was not exclusively male."[13] These persons helped to unify Irish culture: "Members of the learned class were free to move from kingdom to

---

[12] St. Patrick's World, pp 27-28
[13] St. Patrick's World, p 28

kingdom, and were respected throughout the country."[14]   This allowed stories and news to be widely shared, and supported a common culture, much as what occurs whenever diverse communities are exposed to common media.   Assisting in this process was the remarkably high regard that the Irish held for the virtue of hospitality.

While pre-Christian Irish society bore little resemblance to life in the Roman Empire, it was not beyond its influence. There had been some contact between Ireland and the Empire for at least 300 years before the fifth century. The Roman historian Tacitus (55-120 A.D.) wrote the following about Ireland: "The interior parts are little known, but through commercial intercourse and the merchants there is better knowledge of the harbours and approaches."[15]   Over the subsequent centuries, goods from the Empire, and even a few Latin words, become widely known throughout much of Ireland. As the influence of the Empire began to wane in the late fourth century, culminating in the withdrawal of their soldiers from Britain in the early fifth century, some changes began in Irish society. Up to that time, kingdoms would only occasionally join together under larger regional kingdoms. Now, however, with the supply of goods from the Empire cut off, many kingdoms began to both consolidate and expand their communities. This meant emphasizing growth and strength rather than the more passive stability of an extended family. Several enlarged kingdoms attained a measure of dominance, notably under two over-kings who ruled from Tara in the north and Cashel in the south. So began "a drastic reshaping of the old tribal nation into a dynastically ruled province of chiefdoms hierarchically arranged in

---

[14] Patrick the Pilgrim Apostle of Ireland, Máire B de Paor, p 30
[15] Early Christian Ireland, Máire and Liam de Paor, p 25

a pyramid of overlordship within which the process of state creation soon began."[16] It is to this changing culture that Patrick, the first missionary Bishop, would come.

---

[16] St. Patrick's World, p. 34

Chapter Two

St. Patrick and His Mission to the Irish

Considering evangelization in the early Christian centuries, Máire B. de Paor writes, "…with one exception, there was seemingly no organized, concerted effort made to go out and convert pagans, beyond the confines of the Western Roman Empire, until the Benedictine Pope, Gregory the Great, initiated it, in the person of Augustine of Canterbury, in the dying years of the sixth century. Patrick's mission to the Irish pagans was that exception."[17]   In Patrick's life, therefore, we have the earliest opportunity to see how the Gospel was presented in a culture outside of that in which it was born.

We are most fortunate to have some primary source material with which to study Patrick's missionary work, namely, two of his own writings: the *Letter to the Soldiers of Coroticus*, and his *Confession*. The first deals with a pastoral crisis in which some British Christian soldiers had attacked Irish Christians, killing some and kidnapping others. In his authority as Bishop, Patrick writes to formally excommunicate the soldiers for their actions, closing with an expression of hope for their repentance. The second is an apologia in which Patrick answers charges that he is unsuited for his ministry by reviewing his life and work.[18]   Before we turn to his mission, let us look at how he came to become a missionary bishop.

---

[17] Patrick the Pilgrim Apostle of Ireland, Máire B. de Paor, p 23

[18] Traditionally, these writings are divided and numbered into sections or paragraphs. When quoting from them, I will put the section number after the citation, for ease of reference, given that a variety of translations are available. These will appear in parentheses, preceded by **L** for Letter or **C** for Confession – see note 5 for an example.

Patrick was born in Roman Britain somewhere near the western coast. Two sets of dates have been proposed for Patrick's years as bishop in Ireland: 432-461 or 461-493. If the first dates are accurate, he may have been born around 385; if the second are correct, his birth would have occurred around 415. In either case, the influence of the Roman Empire was waning. Rome itself was sacked in 410, and a withdrawal of the military occurred in 420. Patrick's father Calpornius was a decurian, a member of the governing class, and his household included several servants. He was also a deacon, and his father, Potitus, had been a priest. In spite of the religious life in his family, Patrick had not been particularly religious.

When he was about 16, Irish raiders captured Patrick and many others. Patrick was forced into servitude under one of the Irish kings, probably in County Mayo. There he remained for six years, working as a herdsman or shepherd. While carrying out this solitary work, he had much time to reflect, and he began praying in earnest, deeply penitent and entrusting himself to God.

> *"I prayed a number of times each day. More and more the love and fear of God came to me, and faith grew and my spirit was exercised, until I was praying up to a hundred times every day – and in the night nearly as often. So that I would even remain in the woods and on the mountain in snow, frost and rain, waking to pray before first light. And I felt no ill effect, nor was I in any way sluggish – because, as I now realize, the spirit was seething within me."[19]*

His daily discipline as a Christian grew, and sustained him throughout his captivity.

---

[19] in <u>St. Patrick's World</u>, p 99 (C16)

After nearly six years, he heard God communicate to him:

"And it was there in fact that one night, in my sleep, I heard a voice saying to me: 'It is good that you fast, who will soon go to your homeland.' And again, after a short space of time I heard this pronouncement: 'Look! Your ship is ready.'"[20]

Shortly afterward, he fled, traveling in the direction he had understood would lead to the ship. He had to travel some 200 miles over territory of which he likely had little knowledge, nor do we have any indication that he knew anyone along the way. Upon his arrival, he found some men preparing to set sail, and he asked them for passage. After he refused to honor one of their pagan practices, he was not allowed to board ship. However, after he retired to pray for the men, they relented:

"Before the prayer was finished, I heard one of them, who shouted loudly after me: 'Come quickly; these men are calling you.' I returned to them immediately and they began to explain to me: 'Come, we will accept you in good faith. Bind yourself in friendship to us in any way you wish.'"[21]

Following a three-day sea voyage, they traveled over land for 28 days, during which time they ran out of food. The captain addressed him:

"'What's this, Christian? You say your God is great and all-powerful. Then why can't you pray for us? For we are in

---

[20] in <u>St. Patrick's World</u>, p 99 (C17)

[21] in <u>St. Patrick's World</u>, p 99 (C18)

danger of dying of hunger. In fact it's doubtful if we'll see another human being.'"[22]

Patrick replied,

> *"'Trust in the Lord my God and turn to Him with all your hearts – since nothing is impossible for Him – that He may send you today more than sufficient food for your journey – for He has an abundance everywhere.'"[23]*

Suddenly, a herd of pigs appeared, and thus they were provided not only with food, but with something regarded by the Irish as a highly prized delicacy.

The next years in Patrick's life are unclear. We do know that he was able to return home, but he left after some time to train for the priesthood. We do not know where he studied, although Gaul is likely. After some years he was ordained. Again, we are not sure what he did as a priest, but, on a visit home, he received a night vision, in which a man, Victoricus, appeared from Ireland and delivered to him a letter, which bore the heading "The Voice of the Irish."

> *"As I began the letter, I imagined in that moment that I heard the voice of those very people who were near the wood of Foclut, which is beside the western sea* [west of Killala Bay, in Co. Mayo] *– and they cried out, as with one voice: 'We appeal to you, holy servant boy, to come and walk among us.' I was pierced by great emotion and could not read on, and so*

---

[22] in <u>St. Patrick's World</u>, p 99 (C19)
[23] in <u>St. Patrick's World</u>, p 99 (C19)

I awoke. Thank God that after many years the Lord answered them according to their cry.[24]

We are not certain how much time elapsed between this vision and Patrick's return to Ireland. We do know that, with support from a dear friend, he was ordained Bishop and was able to return as a missionary, assuming some level of support from church superiors. We may guess that he was about 46 years old when he arrived in Ireland. Some 25 years had passed between his escape and his return. He was acting in grateful obedience to his Lord, who had been with him throughout his life:

> *"While it was not of my own choice that I arrived in Ireland at that time when I was almost a lost soul, it was a good thing for me, because I was reformed by the Lord and He prepared me to be today what was once remote from me; so that, whereas once I did not even consider my own salvation, now the salvation of others is my care and concern.*[25]

This commitment to leave his family and homeland was costly to him, but he saw it as small compared with the privilege of serving God:

> *"I have sold my patrimony, without shame or regret, for the benefit of others. In short, I serve Christ on behalf of a foreign people for the ineffable glory of life everlasting which is in Christ Jesus our Lord.*[26]

Patrick would spend the rest of his life, some 31 years, in Ireland, eventually so identifying with those who had called him to be with

---

[24] in St. Patrick's World, p 100 (C23)
[25] in St. Patrick's World, p 101 (C28)
[26] in St. Patrick's World, pp 110-111 (L10)

them that he came to describe himself as Irish.[27] Let us now see how this godly bishop spread the Gospel.

Patrick's six years as a slave in Ireland had prepared him in several ways to be a missionary there. First, he learned much from Ireland herself. Most of his time had been spent in rural solitude among the sheep under his care. "Here in the heart of the country, Patrick communed with nature in all her changing moods; here he learned the loving, patient, sensitive, and multi-faceted skills of a good shepherd which were required of him in every season of the year."[28] His dependence upon nature for daily life would have been quite different from what he had known as a member of a wealthy family in Britain, where what had been sport there, now became a matter of survival. This enabled him to develop a sensitivity to the Irish regard for nature, and also to appreciate what Christians believe to be its sacramental character. He may well have meditated often on St. Paul's words in his letter to the Romans: "Ever since the creation of the world his invisible nature, namely, his eternal power and deity, has been clearly perceived in the things that have been made."[29] He also learned that Irish society was hierarchical, and that slaves and outsiders had no social standing. In this way, he could identify with Jesus the Son of Man who had no place to lay his head. He also had enough social contact to have learned the Irish language, and many common religious beliefs and practices. This enabled him to return to Ireland particularly equipped to communicate to the people with sensitivity and understanding. It has often been remarked that the best evangelism must begin with genuine concern and sensitive listening: "Indeed the fact that Patrick understood the

---

[27] in St. Patrick's World, pp 112 (L16)
[28] Patrick the Pilgrim Apostle of Ireland, M.B. de Paor, p 31
[29] Romans 1:20 RSV

people and their language, their issues, and their ways, serves as the most strategically significant simple insight that was to drive the wider expansion of Celtic Christianity, and stands as perhaps our greatest single learning from this movement. There is no shortcut to understanding the people. When you understand the people, you will often know what to say and do, and how. When the people know that the Christians understand them, they infer that maybe the High God understands them too."[30] Patrick's listening continued after he left Ireland, as we have seen with his night vision. This call moved him to compassion, which shows that he went to them with genuine love. Once, as a slave, he had been shepherd to Irish sheep; now, as God's servant, he would shepherd the Irish people, leading them to the Good Shepherd.

An underlying vision of human life in relationship to God permeates Patrick's writings, and he used his own experience as his touchstone: He was a sinner, undeserving of God's grace. Yet, when he turned to God in penitence and need, God blessed him, guiding him to freedom. In response, he chose to return praise and thanks to God, trusting and obedient, sharing this message with others. This is illustrated near the beginning of his Confession:

> *"I was then barely sixteen. I had neglected the true God, and when I was carried off into captivity in Ireland, along with a great number of people, it was well deserved. For we cut ourselves off from God and did not keep His commandments, and we disobeyed our bishops who were reminding us of our salvation. God revealed His being to us through His wrath: He scattered us among foreign peoples, even to the end of the*

---

[30] The Celtic Way of Evangelism, George G. Hunter, pp 19-20

earth, where, appropriately, I have my own small existence
among strangers.

"Then the Lord made me aware of my unbelief, so that –
however late – I might recollect my offences and turn with all
my heart to the Lord my God. It was He Who took heed of my
insignificance, Who pitied my youth and ignorance, Who
watched over me before I knew Him and before I came to
understand the difference between good and evil, and Who
protected and comforted me as a father would his son. That is
why I cannot remain silent (further, it would be inappropriate
to do so) about the great favours and graces which the Lord
deigned to grant me in the land of my captivity. For the way
to make repayment for that revelation of God through
capture and enslavement is to declare and make known His
wonders to every race under heaven."[31]

Being thus rooted in his personal experience of God, Patrick would
have earned a fair hearing by the Irish, for whom testimony was
considered a matter of integrity and courage. Also, Patrick did not
see redemption as merely a personal gift to be enjoyed, but that what
God gave to him, He would give to as many as would receive Him.
So, Patrick's experience of God's redemption came with concern for
any who did not know Christ. The sin from which he had been set
free included any tendency to self-centeredness, which would have
blinded him to the need that others had for God.

While Patrick's faith was deeply personal, it was fully
consistent with orthodox Christian faith. In fact, he seems to have
been aware of the Church's struggles with various heresies, and he

---

[31] St. Patrick's World, p 96 (C1,C2, C3)

taught the Creedal faith with no compromise. A creed-like paragraph is found early in his Confession, and its presence demonstrates that Patrick's mission was no simple invitation to religious experience apart from revealed truth:

> *"Because there is no other God, nor has there been, nor will there be in the future, other than God the Father, begotten without beginning, from Whom all things begin, Who governs all things, as we have been taught; and His Son Jesus Christ. Whom we testify to have been manifestly with the Father always, to have been spiritually with the Father since before the beginning of time, to have been born of the Father before the beginning in a way that cannot be described. And by Him were made things visible and invisible. He was made man. Having vanquished death He was taken back into heaven and earth and hell, so that every tongue should confess to Him that Jesus Christ is Lord and God. We believe in Him and expect His coming in the near future as Judge of the living and the dead, Who will make return to all according to what they have done. He poured out abundantly on us the Holy Spirit, the gift and pledge of immortality, Who makes of obedient believers sons of God and co-heirs of Christ. We confess and adore Him as one God in the Trinity of the Holy Name."* [32]

Patrick believed that the truth had set him free, and his mission would not allow any compromise or abbreviation. Nevertheless, it is interesting to note some peculiar emphases in Patrick's statement that distinguish it from the common Creeds of the Church. First, he pays extraordinary attention to the unique divinity

---

[32] St.Patrick's World, p 96-97 (C4)

of God the Father, as maker of and Lord over all creation, whose Son and Holy Spirit we see in relationship to Him as Trinity. This would have been of paramount importance in communicating to a people who revered all creation, inviting them to recognize the origin of all they saw and did not see but respected and feared. He did not refute their belief in the supernatural character, but affirmed it, showing them that the Creator/God had left witnesses to Him in all His creatures (Rom. 1:20). Also, his simple descriptions of the Incarnation - Christ made man, conquering death, and returning to the Father – would have meant much to people for whom the link between this world and the otherworld was mysterious, and for whom death was the supreme mystery. Of equal importance was the idea that a Holy Spirit would lead us from within to be obedient believers and thus become children of God and co-heirs with Christ. The Irish pagans believed themselves to be susceptible to supernatural influence and possession, and so this Christian belief would both confirm their intuitions and offer hope of trustworthy, effective help. In sum, Patrick's gospel underscored the importance and offer of a personal relationship with the Lord of Creation through Jesus Christ, who would set us free from sin and death, and support us for our journey heavenward by the indwelling guidance of the Holy Spirit – an offer with great appeal to the pagan Irish, both affirming their deepest intuitions and revealing an unexpected but wholly welcome, loving purpose to each person's life.

Another key element of Patrick's message was the importance of personal openness to God, particularly in prayer. We noted that early in his captivity, Patrick came to pray a hundred times a day and nearly as many at night. We also saw that he heard God communicate with him after nearly six years. This implicitly affirms the importance of both repetition and perseverance in prayer. He also experienced and taught that the aim of prayer is not speaking to God, but rather hearing Him, and his experience showed that regular praying enables one to be a more attentive listener. This would be easily understood by the Irish, whose religious practices included a variety of rituals, and whose efforts were designed to help them to be open to the divine. Interestingly, Patrick does not speak of God answering his prayer, but rather that "one night, in my sleep, I heard a voice,"[33] which he knew to be from God. His communion with God deepened over the years, as we see in this remarkable passage, which describes an experience he had before his return to Ireland years later:

> *"And another night He spoke (God knows – not I – whether within me or beside me) in words which I heard in terror, but without understanding them, except that at the end of the message, He said: 'He who gave His life for you; it is He who speaks within you.' And so I woke, full of joy. And again, I saw Him praying within me and I was as if I were inside my own body, and I heard Him above me – that is, over my inner person – and He was praying hard with groanings. And all the while I was dumbfounded and astonished, wondering Who it could be that was praying within me. But at the end of the prayer, He spoke, saying that He was the Spirit. And so I woke, and I recollected what the Apostle had said: 'The Spirit helps us in the deficiencies of our prayers, for we do not now what is proper to pray for, but the Spirit Himself pleads on our behalf with unutterable groanings which cannot be*

---

[33] in St. Patrick's World, p 99 (C17)

26

expressed in words.' And again: *'The Lord, our advocate, prays on our behalf.'"*[34]

Máire B. de Paor wrote concerning Patrick's prayer: "The 'experience of Christ praying in him,' the complete openness to his indwelling Spirit at work in him as a member of the Mystical Body of Christ, is the foundation on which his whole spiritual life is built and the cause of his complete trust in the Lord in all that pertains to himself and to his divine mission."[35] The depth, intensity, and unselfconsciousness of Patrick's intimacy with God, combined with his wholehearted, reverent obedience to His sovereignty, is a rare combination, a characteristic of true holiness, which doubtless attracted many to listen to what he had to say.

Patrick also stressed the personal character of Christian witness. He implicitly taught his converts that one cannot ultimately separate the Christian message from the Christian messenger. Addressing how he was able to carry out his ministry in spite of his many inadequacies, he wrote:

> *"How much more ought we not to aim at that, since, as it is written, we ourselves are 'the letter of Christ for salvation, even to the end of the earth,' and, even if the language does not flow but is blocked and turgid, 'it is written on your hearts not with ink but with the Spirit of the living God.' And*

---

[34] in St. Patrick's World, p 100-101 (C24, 25, including citations from Rom. 8:26 and Heb. 9:24)
[35] Patrick the Pilgrim Apostle of Ireland, p 97

*again the Spirit affirms that rustic backwardness, too, was
created by the Most High.* "[36]

Such humble acknowledgement that God can use us even in our
weaknesses as His witnesses would have been a great encouragement
to his listeners, who knew quite well their own lack of qualifications
for ministry. As a pagan people, newly exposed to the Gospel, they
would certainly have been reticent to believe the Creator could use
them for His work. They would have learned first from Patrick what
St. Paul meant about boasting of one's own weaknesses, glorifying
God thereby. (cf. 2 Corinthians 12:7-9). Late in his Confession,
Patrick writes specifically of some of his weaknesses as bishop,
illustrating again how God entrusts His treasure to earthen vessels:

> *"That is why I should give thanks to God without ceasing –
> because He has often been lenient with my foolishness and
> my carelessness. And because on more than one occasion He
> has not been wrathful with me, who was given to Him as a
> helper but who did not quickly accept the task which was
> made clear to me nor do as the Spirit prompted. And the
> Lord took pity on me countless times, because He saw that I
> was ready, but that I did not know how to organize myself for
> these matters.* "[37]

Patrick modeled the conviction that it is better, when engaged in
God's service, to acknowledge our weaknesses in reliance on God
and others, than to try to hide them, opening us to charges of
hypocrisy. He prepared his Christians to go out, not as experts or

---

[36] in St. Patrick's World, p 98 (C11, including citations from Acts 10:47 and 2 Cor.
3:3)
[37] in St. Patrick's World, p 105 (C46)

professionals, but as amateurs who serve God, whose divine strength is their glory.

Knowing God to be a forgiving Lord, and knowing himself to be a forgiven sinner, Patrick maintained a deep willingness to forgive others, and to pray for sinners' repentance even while reminding them of God's justice. He modeled this most poignantly in his *Letter to the Soldiers of Coroticus*. These nominal Christians had attacked Irish Christians, resulting in the murder of some and kidnap of others, including many women whom they also abused. Early in his letter, he expresses regret that he must write as he does:

> *"I would not have chosen to speak as harshly and as sternly as I must; but the zeal of God compels me, and Christ's truth urges me, for love of my neighbours and children on whose behalf I gave up my parents and my homeland, and my very life until death. If I am worthy, I live for my God to teach the heathen, even if many look down on me."*[38]

He describes the just end of those guilty of such an "unspeakably horrible crime:"[39]

> *"Where then will Coroticus and his most criminal crew – rebels against Christ – where will they see themselves, they who have distributed young Christian girls as prizes, for the sake of a wretched worldly kingdom which will pass away anyway in an instant? Like mere mist of smoke which is dispersed by the wind, deceitful sinners will perish in the face of the Lord; the just on the other hand will feast in perfect*

---

[38] in <u>St. Patrick's World</u>, p 109 (L1)
[39] in <u>St. Patrick's World</u>, p 112 (L17)

harmony with Christ; they will judge the nations and rule over wicked kings for ever and ever. Amen."[40]

Although he justly condemns them for their sin, he is not without concern for them.

"On this account I do not know whom I should lament more, those who were killed or capture, or those whom Satan has so thoroughly ensnared. For they will be consigned along with him to the eternal pains of hell, since he who commits sin is a slave and will be known as a son of Satan."[41]

Even though this is a letter of excommunication, Patrick ends with hope:

"Most earnestly, I ask whichever servant of God may be willing, to be the bearer of this letter, so that no one may for any reason withdraw or hide it, but rather so that it may be read aloud in public, and in the presence of Coroticus himself. Because, if sometime God should inspire them to come back to their sense of Him, and, however late, if they should repent of such unholiness as they committed – murder the Lord's brethren! – and if they should release the baptised prisoners whom they had captured; so may they merit life from God, and may they be restored to wholeness now and forever! Peace in the Father and the Son and the Holy Spirit."[42]

---

[40] in St. Patrick's World, p 112 (L19)
[41] in St. Patrick's World, p 109 (L4)
[42] in St. Patrick's World, pp 112-113 (L21)

Patrick's ability to maintain sharp focus on both God's justice and His mercy simultaneously would have made a deep impression on all who knew him, and would have conveyed a high standard for those who would respond to his mission or carry on as missioners themselves.

An implicit element of Patrick's teaching was the great importance of Scripture. Even when he is not quoting the Bible, his language is rooted in it. In his translation and notes, Liam de Paor cites 35 quotations or direct allusions to Scripture in the *Confession* and 23 in the *Letter*.[43] This is especially noteworthy considering the brevity of the writing, which, in one version readily available, consists of 24 pages.[44] In her in depth analysis of the writings, Máire B. de Paor cites more than 550 Biblical references in the *Confession* and more than 100 in the *Letter*.[45] Patrick certainly encouraged his converts to have an abiding closeness with God's word in Scripture, assuring them, as witnessed by his own use of it in his writings, that it would be of great help in every aspect of their lives. This would have presented a challenge to the Irish, who at that time had no written language. His influence in this regard was so great that the next two centuries would see the creation of incredibly rich libraries in many monasteries, and it was there that Irish came first to be written. Also, many Latin writings were copied and written. Indeed, "The Irish monks were the first Latin writers in the West to comment on the catholic Epistles and Hebrews; between 650 and 800 more than half the biblical commentaries in the West were by Irishmen or their pupils."[46]

---

[43] St. Patrick's World, pp 96-113; 301-303
[44] Patrick in His Own Words
[45] Patrick the Pilgrim Apostle of Ireland, pp 266-275; 294-296
[46] The Archdiocese of Armagh: A History, Msgr. Raymond Murray, p 14

An additional element of Patrick's teaching to consider is his conviction about the fulfillment of prophecy regarding the future and the end of the world. In his *Letter,* he writes,

> *"I am one of those whom He called and predestined to preach the Gospel to the ends of the earth..."*[47]

He understood the New Testament word that this mission must be fulfilled according to Jesus' command to His disciples (cf Matt 28:16-20). This would pave the way for Christ's return, the end of the world, and the fullness of the Kingdom of God. For Christians in Patrick's time, the western edge of the world was Ireland, after which there was only the Western Sea. Moreover, in the fifth century the civilization known to Christians, the Roman Empire, was coming to an end. The sacking of Rome, the "eternal city" by the Goths in 410 was seen by many as the beginning of the end, and by 420 Britain was outside the Empire.

For the pagan Irish, this basic teaching would have offered an explanation for many of their questions regarding the relationship between this world and the otherworld, and would certainly have gotten their attention. However, while Patrick understood his mission as helping in the completion of the Church's work before the End, he worked hard not only in building up the Church through baptisms but also in insuring its future by ordaining priests. This, coupled with his pastoral teaching in general, shows that his conviction regarding the End did not cause him to be preoccupied with the "Last Days" in and of themselves. In his understanding, which was common in the early Church and has been the primary Christian view, these "Last Days" were simply the age of the church, and contained all time between Pentecost (the 50th day following

---

[47] in St. Patrick's World, p 110 (L6)

Jesus' resurrection when the Holy Sprit descended upon the disciples of Jesus – see Acts 2) and the Second Coming of Christ at the end of time. Patrick's convictions did not keep him from caring deeply and personally for his converts, whose ministries he supported as a father would his own children. Their future, whatever would come, was his own. This he expressed in many passages we have looked at, but perhaps never more startlingly than in his impassioned *Letter*. He cries out in sorrow over the treatment of his Christians by the British soldiers:

> *"Perhaps they do not believe that we have been given the same baptism, or that we have the same God. For them it is shameful that we are Irish"[48]*

Patrick, the British son of a government official, sees himself late in his life as an Irishman! Perhaps it is this last fact that most clearly explains both his missionary approach and its remarkable success.

A final missionary priority of Patrick warrants mention, as it had a tremendous impact on the unique form that Church organization would assume in Ireland. It is implicit rather than explicit in his writings. His teaching concerning the importance of the Church centered on the sacraments, faith, scriptures and ministry, and not on its supporting structures. This opened the way for subsequent generations of Irish Christians to adapt such structures to the needs of their distinctive culture. This will be addressed in the next chapter. Here we simply note that it was Patrick's prioritizing of the elements of Christian teaching, which enabled his successors

---

[48] in <u>St. Patrick's World</u>, p 112 (L16)

to distinguish essentials from those matters which could be changed subject to cultural needs.

By any accounting, Patrick's mission among the Irish was enormously successful. As the true apostle of Ireland, all who followed him in mission over the next two centuries owed him a great debt, not least in the way in which that mission was carried out. His central message – that the great Creator of all things, whose majestic authority was visible in all of nature, is surpassingly loving and gracious, and that He has sent His Son into our nature in order that we be set free from sin and united to His divine life – was conveyed with personal integrity in the way he loved and gave his life for them. All future mission would be carried out with the same dedication.

We will close this chapter with a summary passage from the *Confession*, which expresses many of his attributes we have been considering:

> *"Because I owe a great deal to God. He gave me this great boon: that through me many heathen should be reborn in God, and that afterwards they should be confirmed as Christians, so that everywhere clergy should be ordained for a population newly coming to the faith, a population which the Lord redeemed from the ends of the earth, just as He had promised through his prophets:* 'The nations will come to you from the ends of the earth and will say: "How empty are the idols which our forefathers erected and they are of no use"', *and again:* 'I have placed you as a light among the

nations so that you may bring salvation even to the end of the earth.'"[49]

---

[49] in St. Patrick's World, p 103 (L38)

Chapter Three

Monasticism and the Spread of Christianity to All Ireland – 500-700 A.D.

By the time of Patrick's death in the late fifth century, Christianity in Ireland had spread considerably. By his own account, Patrick had baptized thousands, ordained many priests, and, quite probably, given his commitments to both normative Christian practice and the Irish church, ordained bishops as well.[50] The Christian faith, sacraments, scriptures and ministry had been planted deep by his teaching, but not so the supportive structures of the church. While he likely encouraged a diocesan structure, the common organization of the Church throughout the Empire, this seems not to have been forced. "We must remember that Ireland had no tradition of centralized organization which would accommodate a hierarchy of urban and provincial bishops."[51]

Although we lack knowledge of the Irish church in the years immediately following Patrick's death, we do know that in the sixth century it became increasingly centered in monastic communities, which came to eclipse any rudimentary diocesan structure he had laid down. Patrick himself was probably familiar with monastic life from Gaul, and indeed his own life seems to have modeled monastic values. Nevertheless, he was not the primary influence which led to their proliferation: "From France, the monastic movement spread into Britain where Ninian, the early fifth-century apostle of the Picts in what is now Scotland, established a monastery at Whithorn or

---

[50] The Council of Whitby in 664 halted the celtic practice of the ordaining of bishops by a single bishop, in favor of the general Western practice, which required three bishops.

[51] The Church In Early Irish Society, Kathleen Hughes, p 78. Moreover, in the Empire the Gospel was not often taken into rural areas.

Candida Casa...It was here that the most famous monastic founders from the northern half of Ireland received their training...."[52] The Irish monasteries "became the essential element in the structure of the Irish church which for centuries had no territorial dioceses but was governed by Abbots of the great religious houses. The new institution fitted into the existing social system."[53] Although the name monastery is given to all such religious communities in early Ireland, the word may be misleading to our modern minds. While some bore a close resemblance to what we commonly think of – a single-sex community of persons living under religious vows of poverty, chastity and obedience – many were more like enclosed, church-centered villages, whose citizenry included laity and clergy, celibates and families. The development of these monasteries, their variety, and their role in the evangelization of Ireland will be the focus of this chapter. Here, we will see how this adaptation of the church to Irish culture was uniquely suited for this purpose.

Beginning in the early years of the sixth century, a small number of converts, both men and women, desired to live apart from worldly community and dedicate themselves to cultivating the presence of God in an atmosphere of penitence and fasting. They established several communities, usually in remote places, such as Skellig Michael, the westernmost point of Europe about eight miles off the Kerry Coast. Probably inspired by the Desert monastics and the teaching of John Cassian (fourth century), this form of Christian life came to be known as "white martyrdom." While this manner of life was not obviously mission-oriented, we should not assume that

---

[52] Walsh and Bradley, p 53. We should also note that what we commonly think of as the Western monastic tradition begun by St. Benedict (480-547) had no influence on Irish monasticism of this period.
[53] Irish Art In the Early Christian Period (to 800 A.D.), Francoise Hardy, p 21

those who focused their attention on God in this way had no concern for those who did not know Christ. In fact, intercession had always been a high priority for ascetics, in the spirit of Jesus' words "For their sakes I consecrate myself."[54]

However, the dominant type of monastery that spread throughout Ireland in the sixth and seventh centuries was not that of these remote ones, but rather a large, accessible community. Some were founded by wealthy families, and in some cases, family members would become abbot or abbess, with this leadership position being passed down within the family. Many of these large monasteries included men and women, and often only a few members were committed to an ascetic life. Under the abbotical authority, such communities would house a bishop and perhaps several priests. In addition to worship, many activities would take place within the monastery, including education, farming, and a variety of crafts. In both their diversity of activity and their economic self-sufficiency, they served in some ways to Christianize the existing form of social organization common to Irish life. Also, by centering life around the church, they bore witness to God's role in all of life. In this way no radical social change was made; the traditional kingdom structures simply became Christ-centered. This helped pave the way for the Gospel to be heard.

Occasionally, monasteries were founded on pagan holy sites – such as wells, groves, hilltops and rivers. This was not done in a combative, triumphalistic way, however. Rather, it was a means of

---

[54] John 17:19, RSV. When I stood in the oratory on Skellig Michael, looking out the east 'window' above the place where the altar would have been, I was deeply moved by the perspective the monks here would have had, facing not only the direction from which Christ is to return, but also the entire world for which He came.

honoring the intuition that people had that certain places existed where the separation between God and people was especially "thin." "Christianity did not eliminate the supernatural from Irish life; it merely traced it to a different source, so early Christians may well have been willing to take over sites already sacred in popular regard."[55] This policy would have helped Christians to gain a sympathetic hearing among the people.

Some monks and monasteries had a special vocation, it seems, to train missionaries to go forth from Ireland, spreading the Gospel and establishing new monasteries. The first to do so was Colum Cille or Columba (521-597). After establishing monasteries in the north of Ireland, where his family were among the most prominent rulers, he left in 563 and founded a monastery on Iona, a small island off the west coast of what is now Scotland. Monks from his community founded Lindisfarne (Holy Island) off the east coast of Northumbria, and others, and evangelized many parts of what are now Scotland and the north of England. This vocation, the leaving of one's homeland for the purpose of spreading the gospel, came to be known as "green martyrdom." ("Irish spirituality distinguished three kinds of martyrdom: red, the blood shed in time of persecution, white, the choice of penance and fasting, and the green martyrdom of pilgrimage, exile for the love of Christ."[56]) Colum Cille was the first, but one may say that this is also what Patrick had done in leaving Britain to spread the gospel in Ireland. In fact, this vocation is ultimately rooted in the example of Jesus, who left his home at the right hand of the Father for our sake.

---

[55] Celtic Monasticism, Kathleen Hughes, p 30
[56] Archdiocese of Armagh: A History, Murray, p 16

After Colum Cille, the best known of these *perigrinatio por Christo* ("wanderers for Christ") to undertake this calling is Colombanus (543-615). He left the large Irish monastery of Bangor, County Down in 587 and founded monasteries throughout much of Europe. During the sixth and seventh centuries, many such pilgrims went forth, and it has been noted that "It is these wandering Irish monks in exile who were responsible for bringing Christianity to large areas of western and central Europe."[57] These efforts, as they became known in Ireland, certainly added to the corpus of "heroic tales" so highly regarded by the Irish, and would have been an attractive dimension of the sharing of the gospel. Beliefs can always be heard more sympathetically when accompanied by wonderful stories about believers from one's own backyard.

One feature which virtually all Irish monasteries had in common was a scriptorium. Here, not only Scripture but also writings from the Church Fathers and other Latin literature were copied. Additionally, stories from the Irish oral tradition were written down, and scholars contributed new works. Writings were produced in both Latin and Irish, which is doubly fascinating because Latin was never a spoken language in Ireland, and Irish had not heretofore been written. For a people who, before the arrival of Christianity, had no true written language, this new emphasis on literature is nothing less than revolutionary. Moreover, the use of the two distinct languages demonstrates the importance for the Irish church of both remaining in the mainstream of the larger Church and also in reinforcing the native culture.

Related to the scriptorium is the commitment in all of the larger monasteries to education. Learning had always been valued in

---

[57] Celtic Spirituality, Oliver Davies and Thomas O'Loughlin, p 19

the Celtic culture, and monastic schools were founded to provide a breadth of religious and secular studies. In many place these schools were supported by fosterage. "Children fostered in a monastery formed part of the abbot's household and received an ecclesiastical education in a monastic school."[58] This practice of fostering had existed in pre-Christian Ireland, and shows a strong sense of the importance of family. As monasteries came to include this, a high level of trust between the church and the Irish people was both expressed and strengthened. A contemporary Irish priest has highlighted the evangelistic significance of those monastic schools: "The church schools of the monasteries developed in harmony with the secular schools of poetry and Irish learning; the Latin and Irish languages mingled, not only cultivating a love of Holy Scripture and introducing the classical authors but also preserving the native literature, sages and genealogies, and leaving us also, almost incidentally, a beautiful corpus of original occasional verse and nature poetry. The old Irish had a feeling for their ancestors and passed on the pagan literary inheritance without necessarily approving of it. Our modern missionaries are learning today what the old Irish practiced: an understanding of natural good and custom."[59]

In choosing a monastic-centered organization over a diocesan structure, Irish Christians demonstrated their commitment to communicate and live out the gospel in a way that would be most beneficial to their mission. Moreover, even monastic life itself was adapted from its foreign origins, finding styles that were best suited to their environment. "Unlike the Desert Fathers, the Irish monks

---

[58] Celtic Monasticism, Kathleen Hughes, p 9
[59] The Archdiocese of Armagh: A History, Msgr. R. Murray, p 15

from the outset valued letters and learning, and almost from the beginning the Irish monastic movement was a missionary movement."[60]   These communities were also able and willing to incorporate the best features of Irish life. As the late scholar of Irish church history, Kathleen Hughes, wrote: "Pre-Christian society, with its institutions of sick-maintenance, fosterage, and the care of the old, had already some concept of social responsibility: the church, with its rights of sanctuary and laws of protection, attempted to increase public security. The Christian church had embraced all that was congenial in heroic society, its honour and generosity, its splendour and display, its enthusiasm, its respect for learning: in so doing, she had shed some of her classical trappings, and had become a Celtic church. Her strength and weaknesses lay in her full adjustment to her environment."[61]

By the year 700, virtually the entire Irish population had become Christian. At that time, the organization and governance of the Church was almost exclusively monastic. These facts stress the importance of this structural modification on behalf of mission.

---

[60] Early Christian Ireland, M. and L. de Paor, p 52
[61] The Church In Early Irish Society, K. Hughes, p 156

Chapter Four

The Communication of the Gospel in Selected Monastic Writings

As we saw in the last chapter, it was largely through monasteries that the Christian gospel was carried to the remotest corners of Ireland in the sixth and seventh centuries. Although firsthand evidence of personal testimony is lacking, we do have an indirect opportunity to learn something of how the gospel was communicated from the monasteries in the literature that came out of them. While these writings, with the possible exception of the last type to be considered, were directed to Christians rather than pagans, they had missionary impact insofar as they influenced the ordinary believers who may have either been taught by them, or cared for by those under their influence. These persons, then as now, would often be the first encounter that many would have with the gospel. Given the witness of Patrick, who so closely identified the messenger with the message, the character and understanding of these Christians in their daily lives was of primary missionary importance. This underscores, therefore, the value of knowing what they were taught.

In this chapter we will consider examples of four primary types of literature that were produced in abundance in the monasteries of this period: Penitentials, Devotionals, Biblical commentaries, and Hagiographies. It should be noted that this survey is highly selective, and meant only to provide representative samples. Moreover, our look will ignore many features of these writings that are worthy of study, since we are concerned primarily with their impact on mission.

I. Penitentials

During the sixth and seventh centuries, monks from a number of Irish monasteries (including at least one of the perigrini, Columbanus) produced pastoral aids for priests in the treatment of sin, called Penitentials. The form of these writings consisted of an identification of specific sins under a general outline of the major vices, with a prescribed penance for each offense, depending on the standing of the penitent, e.g., bishop, monk, priest who is not a monk, and layperson. Because these lists of sins and penances are so remote from contemporary pastoral practice, regardless of church affiliation, most find them of little use or interest. The most extreme aversion to them was expressed in 1896 by noted historian Charles Plummer: "The penitential literature is in truth a deplorable feature of the medieval church. Evil deeds, the imagination of which may perhaps have dimly floated through our minds in our darkest moments, are here tabulated and reduced to system. It is hard to see how anyone could busy himself with such literature and not be worse for it."[62] However, this assessment surely ignores the forest for the trees, and recent scholars like Kathleen Hughes and Thomas O'Loughlin have provided useful insights into their fundamental role, both in Ireland and for the larger Church.[63] Here, we will not consider the details of sins and penances included in the Penitentials, but concentrate on their primary intent and focus, which offers much of lasting value in addition to shedding light on the pastoral approach which benefited the growing Irish church.

The primary purpose of the Penitentials was to enable priests to provide beneficial and biblically-supported pastoral care to penitent sinners. They were designed to help each sinner to come to

---

[62] quoted in Early Christian Ireland, K. Hughes, p 84
[63] ibid, pp 82-99; Celtic Theology, T. O'Loughlin, pp 48-66.

spiritual health. The Irish monks had learned from the writings of John Cassian (d. 435) who taught that sin and penance should be viewed "medically," seeing sin as disease, sinners as weak, and penance as medicine and therapy. This teaching differed considerably from the prevailing pastoral practice of the early Church, which used a legal analogy in which sin was the breaking of the law, sinners were criminals, and penance was punishment. He also taught the principle learned from Greek medical theory of "healing through contraries."[64] In his sixth century Penitential, Finnian wrote:

> *"By contraries, let us make haste to cure contraries...Patience must arise for wrathfulness; kindliness, or the love of God and of one's neighbour, for envy; for detraction, restraint of heart and tongue; for dejection, spiritual joy; for greed, liberality."[65]*

Confession and penance "were intended to heal the hurt which a man does by his sin; primarily to heal the hurt to himself, and also the hurt to society."[66]

This entire matter of confession and penance refers to sins committed after baptism. This was a problem that Christians had been concerned with since the early years of the church. The Penitentials' perspective represented a significant shift from the general teaching of the theologians. As Thomas O'Loughlin notes in considering the writings of Finnian: "While Patristic theologians could not stop looking backwards in their view of penance, analyzing how a perfection once given in baptism had been lost, Finnian starts

---

[64] Celtic Spirituality, O. Davies and T. O'Loughlin, p 39
[65] in Early Christian Ireland, K. Hughes, p 85
[66] Early Christian Ireland, K. Hughes, p 85

with the facts of imperfect discipleship and asks how it can be repaired, improved, and hastened towards its purpose, so that those who come to him 'can reign with Christ in the life to come, with the holy Abraham, Isaac, Jacob, Job, Noah and all the saints.'"[67] O'Loughlin has also provided a helpful summary of the differences between the Patristic approach and that of the Penitentials:

---

[67] Celtic Theology, T. O'Loughlin, p 59 (quoting Finnian)

"Patristic notions of penance within the church	Assumptions underlying the Penitentials
Once-off unrepeatable event, that must be seen as extraordinary	A repeatable action, seen as part of ordinary Christian discipline
The sin which necessitates penance is a major one, seen as a crime which wilfully breaches the law.	It covers the range of human weakness, seen as the presenting problems of a deeper sickness.
Penitential acts are presented as punitive suffering keyed to the criminal act.	Penitential acts are seen as therapy keyed to the patient and the illness.
There is a distinction between the penitence demanded as part of the decision of discipleship and penance to recover the baptismal condition.	Penance and discipleship are integrated as aspects of ongoing Christian growth to 'the fullness of Christ' at the end of life.
Recovery after the event of penance is a static condition of the soul, focused on the moment of the beginning of Christian life in baptism.	Recovery is a life-long process, focused on the destination of the Christian life when the individual is called into paradise."[68]

---

[68] Celtic Theology, T. O'Loughlin, p 65-66

We can examine each of these assumptions from the Penitentials and see what influence they would have had on Christian mission. The first teaches that Christians are not without sin. So, they would have no illusions about moral superiority. This teaching has become common in most Christian traditions, however much individual Christians may not like to admit it. The second assumption reminds us that our entire human nature is affected by 'original sin,' and our openness to God's forgiving grace must allow Him to reach more deeply into our lives than just the will, where choice lies. It offers a helpful perspective on St. Paul's description of his (and our) condition:

> *"We know that the law is spiritual; but I am carnal, sold under sin. I do not understand my own actions. For I do not do what I want, but I do the very thing I hate. Now if I do what I do not want, I agree that the law is good. So then it is no longer I that do it, but sin which dwells within me. For I know that nothing good dwells within me, that is, in my flesh. I can will what is right, but I cannot do it. For I do not do the good I want, but the evil I do not want is what I do. Now if I do what I do not want, it is no longer I that do it, but sin which dwells within me. So I find it to be a law that when I want to do right, evil lies close at hand. For I delight in the law of God, in my inmost self, but I see in my members another law at war with the law of my mind and making me captive to the law of sin which dwells in my members. Wretched man that I am! Who will deliver me from this body of death? Thanks be to God through Jesus Christ our Lord!"* [69]

---

[69] Romans 7:14-25a RSV

So, this assumption, as the first, presents a realistic appraisal of our condition, which would likely have helped to keep the listener open to hearing more. The third assumption turns our attention concerning discipline for wrongdoing from simple punishment to seeing it as part of healing. This helps address the problem of thinking simplistically of rewards and punishments for our actions. It also helps prevent unhealthy concern with suffering as an end in itself, which has sometimes surfaced in the history of the church, and certainly in pagan society. The fourth assumption encourages the Christian to be patient, allowing the penance and any other suffering to be remedial and purgatorial, encouraging one's health. Since our natural tendency is to experience suffering as punitive, this teaching encourages sufferers to look for something good to come out of it – a useful tool in evangelism. The fifth assumption encourages the grounding of one's life in hope, rejecting unnecessary worry or despair. It offers a helpful slant on St. Paul's words to the Christians in Philippi: "Not that I have already obtained this or am already perfect; but I press on to make it my own, because Christ Jesus has made me his own. Brethren, I do not consider that I have made it my own; but one thing I do, forgetting what lies behind and straining forward to what lies ahead, I press on toward the goal for the prize of the upward call of God in Christ Jesus."[70] In terms of mission, this places the attention of the Christian, whether considering himself or his non-Christian neighbor, not on the past, but on Christ, encouraging him to entrust himself and all people to Him.

Two further elements of the teaching of the Penitentials are important for our purpose, both of which are expressed in the

---

[70] Philippians 3:12-14, RSV

Penitential of Cummean from the seventh century. Like others, it uses the outline of the primary vices, then details specific sins and offers penances depending on one's place within the church. But it is in his Prologue and concluding paragraphs that these important elements are found. First, Cummean reminds his readers at the end of his work that pastoral care when providing penance requires that all circumstances concerning both the sin and the offender must be taken into account:

> *"1. But this is to be carefully observed in all penance: the length of time anyone remains in his faults, what education he has received, with what passion he is assailed, with what courage he resists, with what intensity of weeping he seems to be afflicted, with what pressure he is driven to sin.*

> *2. For Almighty God, who knows the hearts of all and has made us all different, will not weigh the burden of sins in an equal scale of penance, as this prophecy says: 'For dill is not threshed with a threshing sledge, nor is a cart wheel rolled over cummin; but dill is beaten out with a stick, and the cummin with a rod, but bread corn shall be broken small' (Is 28:27-28), or as in this passage: 'The mighty shall be mightily tormented' (Wis 6:7).*

> *3. For which reason a certain man, wise in the Lord, said: 'To whom more is entrusted, from him more shall be exacted' (cf. Lk12:48). Thus the priests of the Lord who preside over the churches should learn that their share is given to them*

together with those whose faults they have caused to be forgiven."[71]

This counsel requires priests to regard each person as unique. He can know best how to prescribe the medicines and therapies, only insofar as he knows the person. One can easily see what a difference this makes when carried out in practice. When a person is really listened to and understood, whatever he or she is told to do is received much more trustingly. Insofar as Irish Christians, thus treated by priests in their own spiritual lives, behaved likewise towards their neighbours, the positive consequences are obvious.

Cummean prefaces his work with a remarkable enumeration of remedies which God provides to heal us from sin, giving a scriptural basis for each:

> "*2. The first remission then is that by which we are baptized in water, according to this passage: 'Unless we are born again of water and of the Holy Spirit, we cannot see the Kingdom of God' (Jn 3:5).*
>
> *3. The second is the feeling of charity, as this text has it: 'Many sins are forgiven her for she has loved much' (Lk 7:47).*
>
> *4. The third is the fruit of almsgiving, according to this: 'As water quenches fire, so too do alms extinguish sin' (Sir 3:33).*
>
> *5. The fourth is the shedding of tears, as the Lord says: 'Since Ahab wept in my sight and walked sad in my presence, I will not bring evil things in his days' (1 Kgs 21:29).*

---

[71] in <u>Celtic Spirituality</u>, Davies and O'Loughlin, p 245

6. The fifth is the confession of crimes, as the psalmist testifies: 'I said, I will confess against myself my injustice to the Lord and you have forgiven the iniquity of my sin' (Ps 32:5).

7. The sixth is the affliction of heart and body, as the Apostle comforts us: 'I have given such a man to Satan for the destruction of his flesh, that his spirit may be saved in the day of our Lord Jesus Christ' (1 Cor 5:5).

8. The seventh is the amending of our ways, that is, the renunciation of vices, as the gospel testifies: 'Now you are whole, sin no more, in case something worse happens to you' (Jn 5:14).

9. The eighth is the intercession of the saints, as this text states: 'If any be sick, let him bring the priests of the church and let them pray for him and lay their hands upon him, and anoint him with oil in the name of the Lord, and the prayer of faith shall save the sick man and the Lord shall raise him up, and if he be in sins, they shall be forgiven him' and so forth, and: 'The continual prayer of a just man avails much before the Lord' (Jas 5:14-16).

10. The ninth is the reward of mercy and faith, as this says, 'Blessed are the merciful for they shall obtain mercy' (Mt 5:7).

11. The tenth is the conversion and salvation of others, as James assures us: 'He who causes a sinner to be converted from the error of his life shall save his soul from death and cover a multitude of sins' (Jas 5:20); but it is better for you, if you are weak, to lead a solitary life than to perish with many.

12. The eleventh is our pardon, as he that is the truth has promised, saying: 'Forgive me and you shall be forgiven' (Lk 6:37).

13. The twelfth is the passion of martyrdom, as the one hope of our salvation then grants us pardon; and God replies to the cruel robber: 'Truly I say to you this day you shall be with me in Paradise' (Lk 23:43). "[72]

The order of these remedies, as well as their content, is revealing. In keeping with orthodox Christian teaching, baptism inaugurates the healing of our sinful nature. By placing love or charity second, "Cummean establishes the priority of the intention of the penitent as a key to forgiveness in general."[73] It also stresses the importance of love in one's life, which "covers a multitude of sins."[74] The third makes a connection between the Christian duty to the poor with healing from sin: "thus he integrates the twin activities of discipleship and forgiveness to an extent the patristic authors never did."[75] The fourth, considering the value of tears, confirms the importance of contrition which has come to be common today but which was not so before Cassian in the western church. We may see this in connection with another Scripture: "the sacrifice acceptable to God is a broken spirit; a broken and contrite heart, O God, thou wilt

---

[72] in Celtic Spirituality, pp 230-231. Cummean's item #1 served as an introduction to the remedies, and therefore was not quoted here.
[73] Celtic Theology, T. O'Loughlin, p 63
[74] 1 Peter 4:8
[75] Celtic Theology, T. O'Loughlin, p 63

not despise."[76] The fifth and sixth confirm the earlier teaching of the church concerning confession and penance, but places them in the context of a larger, gracious program of God for human healing. The seventh stresses the importance of each penitent participating actively in overcoming sin, not simply expecting to passively receive care from without. We have learned how important this is in many aspects of life. One can hardly imagine a physical health program that does not require the individual to participate actively in some way. Once we have accepted the fact that we cannot save or heal ourselves, it is crucial that we learn that there are positive steps we must take in cooperation with divine grace. The eighth makes clear the importance of the Body of Christ, the Church, as a means of conveying grace. This combats the particularly modern tendency for us to see ourselves as utterly independent and self-contained. This point would have had special relevance to the pagan Irish, who had such deep regard for family and community. The importance of mercy in the ninth, and pardon in the eleventh, would have encouraged the penitent to carry forward to others the blessings he has received. This also echoes Patrick's linking of the messenger and the message. The tenth remedy addresses directly the importance of sharing the gospel with unbelievers, the value of which for mission is straightforward. It is unexpected, however, (and inspired, I believe) to see persons encouraged to evangelize as a means of healing the evangelist! The twelfth and concluding aid recognizes the virtue of laying down one's life for God. To put God first in one's life is an explicit way of opening oneself for His cleansing. It was such self-denial that so impressed the Irish pagans about Patrick, and would have surely been appreciated whenever apparent in a Christian's life. Indeed all of these remedies, when

---

[76] Psalm 51:17 RSV

54

received by the penitent, doubtless produced a quality of believing which was instrumental in the successful spread of the gospel to the Irish of this period, as I believe it would be whenever and wherever they are received.

Whatever may be said about the specifics of the sins and penances prescribed in the Irish Penitentials (which we have ignored in this study as irrelevant to our purpose), their pastoral approach and teaching were invaluable in the practical living out of the Christian life in their time and place. Their approach to the treatment of post-baptismal sin not only had an enormous impact on Ireland, but also throughout the western church. Private confession of the individual to a priest who served as an anamchara (soul-friend), providing sensitive, personal care quickly became normative in the early medieval church. Whatever later developments occurred to corrupt the practice in several ways, we cannot on that account dismiss their great value, not least in Ireland herself. As Thomas O'Loughlin writes, "The penitentials were pastorally effective and helped to develop a deeper understanding of the process of life in Christian discipleship."[77]

II. Devotionals – *Aipgitir Chrábaid* – 'Alphabet of Devotion'

Many collections of wise counsels and maxims were produced during the sixth and seventh centuries. While most were especially designed for those living in monastic communities, their influence would have likely gone far beyond them. Unlike the Penitentials, these writings, offering short, often pithy statements, would have been accessible at least in parts, to non-monastic laity. One can imagine a quote from one of these being used in a parochial

---

[77] Celtic Theology, T. O'Loughlin, p 66

sermon and remembered and then used by those who had heard it. We will be looking at only one Devotional here, the remarkable *Aipgitir Chrábaid* or 'Alphabet of Devotion,' one of the oldest surviving documents written in Irish. It is attributed to Colmán mac Beógnai, nephew of Colum Cille (Columba), Abbot of Lynally in Co. Offaly, who died in 611. As scholar and author Dr. John Carey writes, "In the lucid consciousness of its pregnant, interlocking teachings, the *Aipgitir Chrábaid* often approaches the diction of poetry, and indeed some of its sections, with their rhythmic cadences and chains of alliteration, resemble the conservative accentual verse found in Irish legal treatises and heroic sagas. It was clearly intended to sink deep into the memories of those who heard it and, once absorbed, to guide them from within."[78] We will be examining several sections which provide insights with particular value for our concerns.

The work opens with a series of statements in which apparent opposites are combined or connected qualities are divided, serving to convey a balanced, mature and challenging vision of holy living:

> *"Faith together with works,*
> *eagerness together with steadfastness,*
> *tranquility together with zeal,*
> *chastity together with humility,*
> *fasting together with moderation,*
> *poverty together with generosity,*
> *silence together with conversation,*
> *division together with equality,*
> *patience without resentment,*
> *detachment together with nearness,*

---

[78] <u>King of Mysteries</u>, John Carey, p 233. Entire text is on pp 233-245.

fervour without harshness,
mildness together with fairness,
confidence without carelessness,
fear without despair,
poverty without arrogance,
confession without excuses,
teaching together with fulfilling,
climbing without falling,
being low toward the lofty,
being smooth toward the harsh,
work without grumbling,
guilelessness together with prudence,
humility without laxity,
religion without hypocrisy –
all these things are contained in holiness. "[79]

We can see in this passage a description of a holy life, which lays down a challenge to every Christian. His display of complementary virtues and attributes (e.g., "detachment together with nearness") and his insight into ways in which we tend to undermine our virtues (e.g., "patience without resentment") reveals deep practical wisdom. His opening line, "Faith together with works" comes from way before the controversies of the Reformation of the fifteenth and sixteenth centuries, and provides a common sense reminder to converts of any time to embrace both in lives and witness.

The following passage shows an understanding that one's spiritual life is a dynamic activity rather than a static condition. The several qualities described as important help us to look at our spiritual condition with a fresh perspective:

---

[79] in <u>King of Mysteries</u>, p 233

There are four redemptions of the soul:
  fear and repentance,
  love and hope.
Two of them protect it on earth,
  the two others bear it up to heaven.
Fear is an obstacle to the sins which are ahead;
  repentance dissolves the sins which have gone before.
Love of the Creator, and hope for His kingdom:
  it is they that bear it up to heaven."[80]

As in the previous passage, we are given an inclusive vision of the Christian life, involving what may appear to be opposites. By reminding us that the importance of fear and repentance is different from, but not less than faith and hope, our perspective on spiritual growth is enlarged. In terms of how we view or understand others, we are sensitized to see God's blessings at work in a variety of ways, enabling us to be better listeners and witnesses. We can look for which of these qualities may be present in a person and then affirm its value in their religious journey.

The next passage is an insightful survey of vices, masquerading as virtues. This is helpful once again in spiritual diagnosis, especially when applied to ourselves. However, it also is helpful in knowing how best to understand and guide others:

"It is proper that we not let the vices beguile [us] in the guise of the virtues.

  for laxity can beguile [us] in the guise of compassion,
  severity in the guise of righteousness,
  pride in the guise of uprightness,
  unholy fear –

---

[80] in <u>King of Mysteries</u>, p 235

> *which does not protect righteousness,*
> *which does not denounce wrong –*
> *in the guise of humility,*
> *meanness and avarice in the guise of moderation,*
> *arrogance in the guise of chastity,*
> *presumptuousness in the guise of abstinence,*
> *wastefulness and prodigality in the guise of*
> *generosity,*
> *intemperate anger in the guise of spiritual fervor,*
> *feebleness and effeminacy in the guise of tranquility;*
> *hardness and calculation in the guise of steadiness,*
> *haste (?) and flightiness in the guise of genius,*
> *partiality (?) and instability in the guise of flexibility,*
> *laziness and indolence in the guise of detachment,*
> *hesitation in the guise of prudence."*[81]

Given that the sin most frequently denounced by Jesus in the gospels was self-righteousness, this reflection on the subtle ways in which one may be deceived into thinking himself good is of great value. As we saw in Cummean's Penitential, one's witness to the gospel needs to be acknowledged as a means of one's own spiritual healing, and any pretense to self-righteousness will diminish the value of the witness, both to oneself and to the one with whom the gospel is shared. Our next selection makes this thought explicit:

> *"As long as a person is unrighteous, he cannot properly proclaim the truth.*
> *Three things seize upon him then:*
> *boastfulness and pride and anger.*
> *If anyone yields to him,*
> *it awakens boastfulness in him.*

---

[81] in <u>King of Mysteries</u>, p 237

If anyone resists him,

   it awakens anger and pride in him."[82]

The following brief selection advises those who would share the truth what to look for in those with whom they would share:

"With respect to yearning for the truth,

   it is fitting that its requirements be striven for:

      fervour without anger,

      humility without negligence."[83]

We have seen throughout this study the importance for Christian witness of knowing one's audience.   Even as this work has encouraged the Christian to close self-examination, it also reminds us here to carefully examine those with whom we would share. Is their search for the truth limited either by anger towards Christians or others, or by an unwillingness to explore certain avenues, such as Christianity?

The next section provides a set of three questions and answers which we can read as particularly addressed to those who would bear witness or evangelize, and provides a simple examination to help one discern readiness for this ministry. It also reminds them that success in mission is not guaranteed merely by their own faithfulness:

"When is one capable of bearing witness on behalf of the souls of others?

   When he is capable first of bearing witness on behalf of his own.

When is he capable of correcting others?

---

[82] in <u>King of Mysteries</u>, p 238
[83] in <u>King of Mysteries</u>, p 238

When he can first correct himself.
When a person converts his own soul to life, how many souls
could he convert?

> *The people of the whole world: provided that they are*
> *open to correction,*
>> *he could convert them to life so that they*
>> *would belong to the kingdom of heaven.*
> *It is their own resistance to correction, and their*
> *wickedness, and their inconstancy, which exile them*
> *from the kingdom of heaven.* "[84]

Next, we are reminded of the intrinsic character of truth as light, and are shown several types of "darkness" in which one may not have yet fully received it. This also supports the conviction that the gospel is truth, and that all truth is harmonious with it:

> *"As a lamp brings forth its light in a dark house,*
>> *so truth rises in the midst of faith in a person's heart.*
> *When it rises there, it casts out four darknesses:*
>> *the darkness of paganism,*
>> *the darkness of ignorance,*
>> *the darkness of doubt,*
>> *the darkness of sin.*
> *so that there is not room for any of them there.* "[85]

In recognizing what aspect of darkness a person may be under, it helps in discerning what to share, and in what way.

We are then given a description of three types of Christians. This can be seen as another diagnostic tool. Since non-Christians

---

[84] in <u>King of Mysteries</u>, pp 239-240
[85] in <u>King of Mysteries</u>, p 240

tend to judge the faith by its practitioners, this becomes helpful in explaining why not all believers make good witness. It also recognizes the teaching, both here and in the Penitentials, that our spiritual healing does not end with conversion:

> *"Three come to Christianity:*
>> *one of them is within it,*
>> *another is beside it,*
>> *another is at a distance from it.*
> *But they are not equal:*
>> *the one who is within it is better than the one who is beside it;*
>> *the one who is beside it is better than the one who is at a distance from it.*
> *The one who is within it is he who pays three things each day,*
>> *so that he may obtain the life of his soul:*
>> *any good of which he has heard,*
>> *and any good thing which he has seen,*
>>> *he has loved and believed in and fulfilled it.*
> *The one who is beside it is he who renounces the world with his lips and affirms it in his heart.*
>> *He frets (?) over fasting and prayer.*
>>> *He has not declared war upon avarice and stinginess.*
>> *One of his hands is stretched to heaven (?),*
>>> *the other to earth.*
> *The one who is at a distance from it is he who maintains Christians with his wealth,*
>> *but does not practise their customs for as long as he lives;*

he thinks it easier to do so at some other time."[86]
We can see that this variety is found among Christians in our churches today. Whether recognizing that this was the case in the early church as well as today is reassuring or disappointing is a matter of perspective, but, as we saw earlier, the truth is always vital to genuine Christian living, and so we accept this for what it is.

The next section appears to be in a catechetical format, putting forth important teachings about basic components of Christian living in a simple setting. Taken to heart, this section provides primary guidance for Christians in their daily lives and, implicitly, in their witness:

> *"The three enemies of the soul:*
> > *the world,*
> > *and the Devil,*
> > *and a sinful teacher.*

> *Three things which drive out the spirit of instability, and make the mind steadfast:*
> > *vigil,*
> > *and prayer,*
> > *and labour.*

> *The four foundations of piety:*
> > *patience to withstand every desire,*
> > *forbearance to withstand every wrong,*
> > *asking pardon for every deception,*
> > *forgiving every sin.*

---

[86] in <u>King of Mysteries</u>, pp 240-241

Four teachings for which we should strive, even if we do not
fulfil them:
> *devotion to God,*
> *gentleness to men,*
> *good will to every person,*
> *expecting death each day.* [87]

Our final selection reminds us that God makes a variety of appeals to persons to lead them to Himself.

"Four things through which the kingdom of God may be
sought:
> *steadfastness and detachment from the world,*
> *devotion and constancy.* [88]

Each of these things may attract one away from this earth-bound life, and lead them in the direction that ultimately goes towards God Himself. If the Christian witness can allow himself to see any of these as intrinsically positive, then the sensitivity necessary for effective evangelism will be matched by an ability to affirm the direction of one's life in such a way as to encourage further growth.

As exemplified by this nearly 1400-year old devotional aid, we can see that the Christian life presented to the Irish people was shown to be central to the whole of life, affecting everything. At the same time, we see that a caution was raised against any tendency to oversimplify either Christian life or growth, whether for oneself or for others. Anyone who would share the gospel with others is

---

[87] in King of Mysteries, p 241
[88] in King of Mysteries, p 243

reminded that he or she would be the first means by which Christianity would be judged, before the message itself would likely be heard, and thus to tend to one's own relationship with God continually. The missionary is also reminded that God reaches people by various means, and therefore must make an effort to discern what He may already be doing in those with whom the gospel would be shared. This "positive evangelism," implicitly taught by such remarkable writings as the *Aipgitir Chrábaid*, was certainly an important element in the successful conversion of the Irish, and may indeed prove important as Christians in the west today face the challenge of presenting the gospel to a different culture than that which has dominated for hundreds of years.

III. Biblical Commentaries – "On the Miracles of Holy Scripture"

As we noted in our remarks on the importance of Scripture for Patrick, those Christians who followed him exhibited a deep devotion to it, resulting in the production of a prodigious number of commentaries (see note 47). The Bible was indeed central to monastic life: Read in daily prayers in the churches, copied in the scriptoria, taught and studied in the schools, written about by scholars. Their many commentaries are just now in the early stages of being edited, and most are as yet not available in English translation. However, recent scholars have made some observations about them. Owen Davies, in his introduction to sources in the anthology Celtic Spirituality, writes that "the general trend seems to be Alexandrian, with a strong emphasis on free or allegorical readings of texts...but in a way that typifies the eclecticism of early Irish Christian culture, the tradition of exegesis of the Psalms was deeply Antiochian (i.e., historical) and closely reflected the commentary of Theodore of Mopsuestia, which survives entire in a manuscript of Irish provenance."[89] This diversity in interpreting suggest an openness of approach to Scripture which encouraged each student to read prayerfully, allowing God to reveal His truth, which in turn could be apprehended and understood in a variety of ways. It also implies that scholars and teachers did not impose a simple, definitive interpretation of texts on their students.

The text that we will be looking at in this study comes from a flourishing school of exegesis in southern Ireland. Augustinus Hibernicus wrote "On the Miracles of Holy Scripture" in 655 at a monastery in Co. Waterford.[90] It consists of three parts: miracles in the Pentateuch, in the remainder of the Old Testament, and in the New Testament.[91] We will be looking at two important themes from the first part which reveal an approach to Scriptures which have missionary consequences: First, the commitment to understand the miracles of the Bible not as capricious interruptions of nature (with the implicit denigrating of nature) but as consistent with reflecting an aspect of God's respect of and authority over His created order; second, the belief that reason is compatible with revelation in discerning the truth.   These both have importance for the Irish mission.

Augustinus Hibernicus begins his work with a reminder that God's miraculous authority is demonstrated in creation:

> *"Since we wish, with the help of almighty God, to treat of those things which are miraculous, where better can we turn for a beginning than to that Creator of all things to whom*

---

[89] Celtic Spirituality, Davies and O'Loughlin, p 52
[90] cf. King of Mysteries, J. Carey, p 51
[91] cf. King of Mysteries, J. Carey, p 51

66

Scripture often bears witness, saying 'He does great and inscrutable deeds, and miracles without number' (Job 9:10)? He established a first foundation, as it were, for all of these miracles when he made all of his creatures out of nothing."[92]

As Dr. John Carey remarks, "Existence itself, then, is the ultimate miracle: had our eyes not grown so dull, they would be dazzled with ineffable wonder wherever we turned our gaze."[93]

Part One continues to comment on the Creation in Genesis. One of the real concerns in our time is the apparent conflict between belief in Creation and the theory of Evolution. Setting aside the specifics of the contemporary debate, it is noteworthy that a form of this issue was taken up in the seventh century. Our author addressed the question of how Genesis 1 can be reconciled with the appearance of new forms of life. His treatment, borrowed in part from St. Augustine of Hippo, is profound and challenging:

"On the sixth day he completed his work on the natures of created things, but even now he does not cease to govern them; and on the seventh day, he rested from the work of creation, but he never ceased from the exercise of government. For we are to understand that God was a Creator then, but is a Governor now. Therefore if among created things we see anything new arise, God should not be thought to have created a new nature, but to be governing that which he created formerly. But his power in governing his creation is so great that he may seem to be creating a new

---

[92] in <u>King of Mysteries</u>, J. Carey, p. 52
[93] <u>A Single Ray of the Sun</u>, J. Carey, p 72

nature, when he is only bringing forth from the hidden depths of its (existing) nature that which lay concealed within.[94]

Considering that science has yet to produce definitive evidence of trans-species evolution, this concept is quite interesting. The text also addresses the problem of time in the matter of creation:

> *"Although it is said that the whole creation was arranged in the course of six days, this does not refer to the succession of days in an interval of time, but to the sequence of (God's) acts. For he who subsequently told the story divided in speech what God did not divide in the perfection of his work."*[95]

Whatever value these thoughts may have had for mission in seventh century Ireland, they certainly are rich and suggestive for our time and culture.

Augustinus treats a number of the miracles of Moses, and we will examine three. Concerning the miracle of the appearance of the burning bush to Moses (Ex 3), he offers an explanation that confirms his commitment to confining the miraculous to being within natural law. Before considering this and other particular miracles, we should remember that his purpose in doing so was not the post-Enlightenment reason of debunking the supernatural. Dr. Carey writes, "Augustinus Hibernicus's stance is precisely the opposite of this: for him, to act against nature would be unworthy of God, and to provide natural explanations for miracles is a way of honouring the Creator."[96] Regarding the burning bush, Augustinus offers two

---

[94] in <u>King of Mysteries,</u> p 52-53
[95] in <u>King of Mysteries,</u> p 53

[96] <u>A Single Ray of the Sun,</u> J. Carey, p 50

possible explanations, either of which, given the science of his day, would reveal the miracle to be 'natural':

> *"It is related that a certain shrub has the property that, the more it burns, not only is it not consumed, but in burning it is purified. Concerning this wood Saint Jerome, in the course of explaining the wooden altar which is described in the city shown by the Lord to Ezekiel in a vision, mentions that its colour is like that of linen; but although he describes its nature, he does not give its name. If the fire shown to Moses was burning in a bush of this kind, what wonder if it was not consumed? For thus the nature of each, of the fire and the wood, is preserved: for the fire burns naturally from the wood, and the burning wood is naturally not consumed by the fire. Or else, to be sure, it was not the fire, which is wood's enemy which appeared in the bush, but rather that fire of which it is said that 'He makes his angels spirits, and his ministers a burning fire' (Psalm 103:4). Thus it is an incorporeal fire which is described in the bush – which, when shown to a fleshly man, must of necessity be revealed as if it were some bodily substance."*[97]

It is worth noting that Augustinus' convictions about miracles led him to search the Scriptures for guidance in understanding. This is in strong contrast to the modern tendency to either deny the miracle altogether or to use the literal, unexamined miracle as a litmus test of real faith.

---

[97] in <u>King of Mysteries,</u> p 57. Carey points out that his text of Jerome was defective, which rendered his effort noble but unnecessary.

For our second miracle of Moses, we turn to the brief treatment of the hand of Moses which was able to alternate between being healthy and leprous (Ex 4). In his explanation, Augustinus offers a view of human nature, which addresses all human conditions, including any miraculous healings or other alterations that occur. It may be that his view is of greater interest today than it was at the time of its writing, given the profound advances in medicine, the growing appreciation and study of non-Western medical care, and the renewal of interest in the ministry of healing among Christians. Again, he assumes that nothing in this miracle was contrary to nature:

> *"For the nature of human flesh has both leprosy and health latent within it, as is often shown by their alternation; but so sudden a change, with a hand appearing in the same moment whole, then white with leprosy, and then again whole, appears to those who behold it as a most miraculous sign."*[98]

The final miracle we will consider is presented in greater length. In treating the apparent conversion of the staffs of Moses and the Egyptians into serpents (Ex 4,7), he expands his view of the impossibility of natures being altered, which includes an explicit word to Irish pagans, and thus is of particular significance for our purpose. He also demonstrates our second consideration raised earlier, the conviction that reason and revelation are ultimately harmonious in the pursuit of truth. Patient inquiry, employing both the deposit of revelation and the function of reason, trusting that all truth is of God, is modeled well here, and, if we study scripture and

---

[98] in <u>King of Mysteries,</u> p 57

come to different understandings today, it is only because we have access to more information.

"The staff changed into a serpent, and the serpent changed back again to wood, constitute a problem for those who inquire into nature – unless it be that each, the staff and the serpent, appears to be made from earth; for being made from the same material, they could by the power of God the Governor be changed into each other by turns. But if it be conceded that all things made from earth can be changed into one another by turns – as for instance animal to tree, bread to stone, man to bird – then none of these could remain firmly within the bounds of its own nature. We would seem, indeed, to give our assent to the laughable tales told by the druids, who say that their forebears flew through the ages in the form of birds; and in such cases we would speak of God not as the Governor, but as the Changer of natures. Far be it from us to do so, lest we believe that after the first establishment of the natures of all things he made anything new, or not contained by its own nature. For 'there is nothing new under the sun,' nor can anyone say 'Behold, this is new' (Ecclesiastes 1:9-10).

Therefore many learned men say rather that the real staff, which as long as Moses held it in his hands was wood, was on various occasions changed into a serpent in appearance only, to serve as a sign – especially when it served no function save that of providing a sign. For if it had truly been a serpent, it would have remained a serpent after the sign was given. Thus it was a real staff with which Moses began to scourge Egypt with plagues, with which the sea was divided, with which the rocks were struck in Horeb and

Kadesh: never changed into a serpent, it remained a staff always.

If then what appeared as a sign was only an imaginary serpent, why were those other serpents of the wizards devoured by it in Pharoah's presence? To this objection the learned have an easy answer: the serpents which it devoured were also imaginary; and so the apparition of the divine portent was able to devour the appearance brought about by the devilish incantation of the wizards.

According to this view, then, the staff was not changed into a serpent's nature but only – in appearance, and as a sign – into its similitude. For nothing can be found in the nature of wood which could make a snake. For this reason that which was by its nature a staff only appeared as a serpent at the time when the sign was given."[99]

As we have seen, the pagan Irish had a deep conviction regarding the sacredness of creation: Their superstitions and other religious practices expressed not only devotion but also bondage. When nature is understood as a closed system, its "laws" have a ruthless quality which coldly demand slavish obedience. In order for the gospel to be welcomed by them, it had to both honor their devotion and yet free them from their bondage. In works such as the one we have been considering this balance is attempted, and, in many ways, achieved. One more passage from Augustinus shows how far a Christian could go in affirming pagan intuition, and, although it does not present the Creator in this specific text, His authority has been implicit throughout, and made most clear in the passage concerning creation with which we opened this survey. Like

---

[99] in <u>King of Mysteries</u>, p 58

several we have considered, the idea expressed here has particular value for our time, as we wrestle with issues concerning our environment. In fact, the chapter in Dr. Carey's book in which this selection is found is entitled "The Ecology of Miracles"[100]. Augustinus wrote,

> *"There is no doubt but that the earth has an unconscious life, through which the foliage of the trees and plants which grow in it can be seen to be moved. And just as throbbing veins of blood run through living flesh, so streams of living water flow through the earth."[101]*

The themes which we have looked at in Augustinus Hibernicus' On the Miracles of Holy Scripture have always been important for Christian mission, and we have seen that, in some instances, his speculations have much to commend themselves to contemporary thought. Certainly, the belief that God the Creator loves, governs, and respects His creation, honoring the boundaries with which He has defined each creature, is as relevant today as it was in reaching out to the pagan Irish. He challenged them to think more deeply about their own beliefs, and, as he revealed contradictions within their own views such as the idea of the alteration of men into birds, he challenged them to give Christianity a fair hearing.

IV. Hagiographies – "The Life of Patrick" by Muirchú

A Hagiography is the life of a saint. This form of literature served a variety of purposes in the early Church. While some

---

[100] A Single Ray of the Sun, J. Carey, pp 39-73
[101] A Single Ray of the Sun, p 64

historical value is intended, this is secondary to their primary purpose, which is to inspire: "The aim of the hagiographer is to communicate with his audience in such a way that they are moved to identify themselves in various ways with the saint, and thus to become imitations of the saint (i.e., become one with the saint in their here and now, rather than some sort of moral imitation.). A parallel is the gospel genre where the intention of the evangelist is to elicit identification with the risen Christ, and it is in support of that aim that we learn of the biography of Jesus."[102] In this way "They function as a catechetical tool."[103] This type of literature began to appear in Ireland in the second half of the seventh century. Lives of each of the three patron saints of Ireland, Patrick, Colum Cille and Brigit, were written before 700, and, in Patrick's case, more than once. We will be looking at a portion of the most famous biography of Patrick by Muirchú, probably written before 688. Muirchú's interest was clearly evangelical, since his audience was being encouraged to identify with the great missionary, and thus continue in the spreading of the gospel in their own time and place. His primary focus is on the relationship between paganism and Christianity. As Oliver Davies writes, introducing the work in the anthology, Celtic Spirituality, "Muirchú has a developed sense of the relationship between Christian revelation and the pagan religion of his ancestors. That religion was not simply a darkness, but a preparation for the gospel, and hence his people were always in some relationship with the true God and under the protection of his Providence."[104]

---

[102] Celtic Theology, T. O'Loughlin, p 87, note 3
[103] Celtic Spirituality, O. Davies, p 27
[104] ibid, p 29

The centerpiece of Muirchú's account is a two-scene act near the Hill of Tara, the religious center of the strongest pagan kingdom in Ireland in Patrick's time. This made it also the symbolic and sacred center of pagan power. Taking place on the night of the Pasch, and again after dawn on that same Easter Day, it tells of the challenge to paganism that Christianity presents.

> *"On the same night on which Patrick celebrated Easter, they [King Loiguire of Tara and his people] conducted their festival of heathen worship. Moreover, they had the custom – proclaimed to all – that whoever in all the country, far or near, should kindle a fire before the fire in the king's house was lit (that is, in the palace of Tara) should be put to death by his people.*

> *"Patrick, then, lit the divine fire – truly bright and blessed – which was seen by the people living throughout the plain. It happened that it was seen from Tara, and at the sight they gazed and wondered. Calling together the elders, the king said to them: 'Who is it who has dared to commit this crime in my kingdom? He must die.' And they all replied that they didn't know who had done this. The druids answered:*

> *'Eternal life to you, King! The fire that we see, which has been lit tonight before the fire was kindled in your house: unless it is extinguished on this same night in which was lit, will not be put out forever. It will indeed rise above all our customary fires; and he who has lit it – along with the kingdom that is arriving through kindling of the fire tonight – will overcome us all and will lead astray all the people of your kingdom; and all the kingdoms will yield to him, and his*

realm will expand over all, and he will rule forever and ever.[105]

We make particular note of the testimony to the power of the gospel offered by the druids. By putting such words and ideas into these pagan leaders, Muirchú is using the model of the apostle, who showed how the prophets of the Hebrews herald the coming of the Messiah (cf. Acts 2:14-36).

Then, taking his druids and other followers with him, Loiguire went to confront Patrick. Waiting beyond the light of Patrick's fire, when Patrick came to them, they refused to rise (except for one of the druids, who was thus blessed for his faith, and whose relics later became venerated), and their disputation began. After hearing Patrick pray, Loiguire ordered him killed, at which Patrick said,

> *"May God come up to scatter His enemies and may those who hate Him flee from before His face."*[106]

At once, the darkness deepened, an earthquake occurred, and only the King and a few survivors were left to return to Tara at dawn.

That morning, Easter Day, Patrick and a few of his followers entered the banquet hall at Tara during King Loiguire's feast with his people. The king invited him to stay, to see what would happen. He accepted, but refused to share the pagan feast. In a scene reminiscent of Moses with the Egyptians in Pharoah's court (Ex 7, etc.), a display of supernatural abilities ensued. Some time later, in a scene

---

[105] in <u>St. Patrick's World</u>, p 183
[106] in <u>St. Patrick's World</u>, p 183

reminiscent of Daniel in the fire (Daniel 3), a druid, and one of Patrick's companions, covered by Patrick's chasuble, were placed in a hut, which was then set ablaze, and afterwards only the chasuble and Patrick's companion were spared. Attempting then to kill Patrick, the king's hand was stayed:

> *"Holy Patrick said to the king: 'If you do not believe now, you will die on the spot; for the wrath of God descends on your head.' And the king, shaken in his heart, feared greatly, as did the whole city with him. King Loiguire summoned his elders and his whole council, and said to them: 'It is better for me to believe than to die.' And he took the advice of his company and followed it: he believed on that day and turned to the eternal Lord God. Many others also believed on that day."[107]*

This is not perhaps the best motive for becoming Christian, but Muirchú was writing to inspire missionary work and convince pagans, not to give spiritual direction. Its popularity, along with the Christianizing of Ireland and the end of the pagan practice, attest to its success. In all of the hagiographies of the Irish saints, we can see a similar appeal, and with similar effect. More popular (and for a more popular audience) than the other types of writings we have been considering, these saints' tales continue to be well-known. In fact, the "Patrick" best known to Christians today is not the man we see in his writings, but the one found in Muirchú and other hagiographies.

---

[107] in <u>St. Patrick's World</u>, p 187

As we have seen in this chapter, a variety of monastic writings were produced which played a part in the Christianizing of Ireland. We have not been able to consider the role of art in this missionary period. Most of the great Irish Christian art would appear beginning in the eighth century, and a basis for studying the few earlier works for this purpose is insufficient. Thus, this sample of Irish religious writing will have to suffice, knowing that many other factors were certainly involved in the process of conversion.

Before concluding this study, we may wish to consider briefly what happened in the Irish church following the period of conversion. It is noteworthy that the most important development in the eighth century was a reform movement! In one sense, conversion is always personal, and therefore, evangelization is a process that never ends. Nevertheless, once the Christian religion came to dominate Irish life, the focus for spreading the faith changed. In the reform efforts by the monks of the Céili Dé (=servants of God) who came from many different monasteries, the attempt was made to address a laxity which had begun to set in within the religious communities. This reminds us that spiritual growth is a journey that has no end this side of heaven, and therefore must be cultivated daily. As we have seen, conversion has a beginning, but no end in this life. Therefore, the Christianization of the Irish really only completed its beginning by the eighth century. From that time on, however, need was not primarily for mission, but for renewal. Thus, the later works produced in Ireland served a somewhat different purpose than that served by the works of the period we have been examining.

Conclusion

The complex factors that contributed to the remarkably smooth, violence-free conversion of the Irish from paganism to Christianity have been only briefly explored in this study. We have noted that the primary element in the spreading of the gospel is the messenger, and we have virtually no record of personal testimony from early Ireland. As a consequence, we have only been able to examine a few written sources of Christian teaching and example. Nevertheless, the texts we have looked at shed significant light on how the gospel was communicated during this unique period.

We began this study with the suggestion that the Irish experience reveals some useful insights or trajectories for contemporary Christians to consider in the mission to our changing culture. Now, we will close with a consideration of several aspects of the Irish experience in this regard. We will look at three exemplary elements, and then three ways in which accommodations were made to existing Irish culture, recognizing also that some aspects of that culture had to be rejected.

Central to the gospel's proclamation in Ireland was the conviction that the Lord and Creator of all things, whose providence oversees all things, who uses every circumstance as a place in which His guidance is manifest, and whose presence is everywhere, has entered into human nature, and lives within everyone who receives Him. Patrick saw God's redemptive will expressed to him when he was enslaved, in exile, and not committed to Him, and this allowed him to see God not as mechanically controlling events but rather as making His grace available in all that happens. This conviction was further modeled in Colum Cille and the peregrini, and was at the root of the guidelines for self-examination and witnessing in the *Aipgitir Chrábaid*. The challenge to our contemporary mission presented by the Irish experience is best rooted here. Although the dominant view in contemporary Western culture is of a closed nature in which everything that happens either reflects natural laws or human action, many people seem to have an intellectual "soft spot" for some kind of benevolent and personal providence. The enormous popularity of J.R.R. Tolkien's The Lord of the Rings, a work soaked through with such a view of providence, bears testimony to this yearning in our time to believe that we are somehow being guided toward an ultimate blessing. In that work, each person invited to join in the mission to deliver the Ring is enabled to see that he has been prepared for this journey all his life. Each one is promised that his acceptance of this personal call, this willingness to pursue it in the company of others, will both ennoble him and serve the good. These virtues transcend all concerns about success and failure. In Patrick, we see one whose confidence in benevolent providence was based on a deep intimacy with his Lord. During his period of servitude, he did not merely experience God's guidance through circumstances and events, but also by His coming to him personally in both prayer and daily life. Later, he taught God's active and personal role in becoming Incarnate and working for our salvation actively from within our nature. His successors equally affirmed that this intimate providential initiative God took in Christ, He offers to us. Many have said that our deepest human need is for intimacy, and yet we have all experienced limitations in personal relationships. We also have recognized that, in our culture, various forms of alienation and feelings of being misunderstood are virtually epidemic. Both as individuals and as a species, we find ourselves out of harmony with others, with our environment, and within ourselves. The union with God to which Patrick testified helped him to live in harmony with all of these components. His example and that of the others we have considered in this study offer an appealing witness which many in our time would find immensely attractive.

The second element to consider is in some ways a complement to the first: the importance of the Church, the Body of Christ, as that unified community into which the individual believer is incorporated. The teaching that God is both One and also Trinity affirms and guides the pagan Irish intuition of the mysterious link between the individual and the community. The sacraments of the Church, the centerpiece of the common life of the faithful, convey and strengthen the double intimacy of believers with God, and with one another. Baptism establishes the mutual indwelling of believers and Christ, and between all baptized in Christ. In the Eucharist, these intimate connections are strengthened as the baptized receive the Body and Blood of Christ in the consecrated bread and wine. The rite of Ordination and the Marriage Blessing enhance these links in practical terms as the common lives of believers and families are assured of the divine Presence. Also, the unifying elements of common faith and scriptures are crucial for the definition of the Christian as a member of the Body of Christ.

This communal component was at the center of the appeal and spread of the monasteries, affirming as they did the intrinsic Irish values of family and community. In our time, these qualities have been largely overlooked in favor of a concentration upon the rights of the individual. Indeed, many in our culture, if asked whether the primary component of society was the family or the sovereign individual, would probably choose the latter. And yet, our needs for family and community do not go away. The paradox that love is other-directed and yet brings self-fulfillment is something that Christians of our time need to teach and live more effectively if our witness is to be received. However, we ourselves are often reluctant to defer to others, personally, parochially, and denominationally. At the Council of Whitby in 664, Celtic Christians were challenged to lay down their peculiar customs, which, through no intention of their own, came to set them apart from the mainstream of the Church. They relented, having no desire to be eccentric. What sort of witness would be made if such considerations were taken to heart in ecumenical, and indeed in denominational and parochial discussions today?

The final component to be considered is the importance of love and understanding in Christian witness. We have seen consistently, from the example of Patrick, referring to himself as one of the Irish, from the counsel to priests in the Penitentials to examine the circumstances of the individual, and from the *Aipgitir Chrábaid's* guide for self-examination, the importance of listening to, understanding, and caring for those with whom one would share the gospel. This is crucial because of the fundamental connection between the messenger and the message: How can the God we represent be taken seriously as One who loves us and wishes to fulfill our deepest needs if we show neither genuine interest nor sensitivity to one another? This also carries with it the importance of allowing everything that one has believed or experienced to be considered proto-evangelical. Keeping in mind the view of divine providence we considered above, the Irish monks were outstanding in their openness to seeing their heritage as preparing the people for Christ: "Just as Eusebius had composed his Chronicle showing how the great world kingdoms of Assyria, Egypt, Palestine and Greece had prepared for Christ, now the *fer comgne* [converted Bards] prepared their column, knowing how all Irish history, from the creation, fitted the same pattern."[108] This attitude respects God as Lord, both of all creatures and also of each individual, and considers that a person will listen to a Christian share Christ because God has been preparing him. The importance of this is great for the challenge Christians face today, and what is required is both greater trust in God and greater openness towards others.

There are at least three ways in which Christianity adapted to Irish culture. Perhaps the biggest from our perspective is the way Patrick and his successors assented to the high view the Irish had of nature. The church in the Roman Empire, for good and pastoral reasons and with the support of the dominant view in Scripture, was strongly anti-pagan. Christians were rightly concerned with the many unnatural practices found among nature worshippers, including infanticide, mutilation and cannibalism, and could not make any compromises with such. In contrast, the pagan Irish were less "unnatural," and, although some beliefs and practices had to be rejected, much was affirmable as compatible with the gospel. In teaching the sacramental character of nature – that, created by God, it could reveal his glory – the Irish monks preceded the rest of the Western church by several hundred years, when St. Francis of Assisi and St. Thomas Aquinas, both considered quite controversial in their time, expressed this in sublime ways. The following passage, from the seventh century hagiography, Bishop Tirechán's "Account of St. Patrick's Journey," illustrates some of the genius of the Irish approach. In it, Patrick is met at a well by the two daughters of King Loiguire, where they have gone to do their washing. They ask him to tell them about his God:

---

[108] Celtic Christianity: Ecology and Holiness, ed. Christopher Bamford and William Parker Marsh, p 20

"Our God is the God of all people, the God of heaven and earth, of the sea and of the rivers, the God of the sun and the moon and of all the stars, the God of the high mountains and of the deep valleys. He is God above heaven and in heaven and under heaven, and has as his dwelling place heaven and earth and the sea and all that are in them. His life is in all things; he makes all things live; he governs all things; he supports all things. He kindles the light of the sun; he builds the light and the manifestations of the night; he makes wells in arid land and dry islands in the sea, and he set the stars in place to serve the major lights. He has a son who is coeternal with him and of like nature. The Son is not younger than the Father nor the Father than the Son; and the Holy Spirit breathes in them. The Father, the Son and the Holy Spirit are not separate. Truly, now, since you are daughters of an earthly king, I wish that you will believe and I wish to wed you to the king of heaven."[109]

As the account continues, we learn that they did become believers and were baptized.

Christians need to be sensitive to the intuitions of today's neo-pagans, and engage them in questioning, trying to examine their convictions in the light of our faith, affirming where we can and denouncing when we must. In the simplest sense, problems emerge wherever created things are valued apart from their creator, and reverence towards them then leads to irrational and unwholesome behavior. In our modern secular culture, similar problems have emerged when we have valued such things as worldly security and material acquisition, apart from their connection with God, before

---

[109] in <u>St. Patrick's World</u>, pp 163-164

whom all earthly goods are merely temporary. In the entire question of how nature/creation is to be regarded, we have one of our greatest contemporary issues. We may remember the words of Pope Gregory the Great to his English missionaries in the early seventh century, as reported by Bede in the eighth:

> *"I have decided after long deliberation...that the idol temples (of the English) should by no means be destroyed, but only the idols in them. Take holy water and sprinkle it in these shrines, build altars and place relics in them. For if the shrines are well built it is important that they should be changed from the worship of devils to the service of the true God."[110]*

Patrick was also willing to make accommodation to Irish social structures. This was difficult for him as a non-native with no rights. In allowing himself to conform, therefore, he must have thought often of the vision in which he was asked by the Irish people to walk among them (Ch. 2, C23). Two features of that life would have been particularly challenging: the strict, hierarchical delineations, and the practice of slavery. Presumably he found scriptural encouragement in such passages as Romans 13:1: "Let every person be subject to the governing authorities. For there is no authority except from God, and those that exist have been instituted by God." Both Patrick and those who continued the Christian mission after him worked within these constraints, sharing the Gospel without challenging the social structure. This accommodation challenges Christians in today's Western democracies in a different setting. In seeing what once was a more Christian-centered culture move away from these roots in favor of a

---

[110] in <u>Celtic Monasticism</u>, K. Hughes, p 31

pluralistic approach to different beliefs, and while moral teachings and laws are changing away from traditionally Christian standards, some Christians are seeking to "take back" control of the government, while others are adjusting their own religious teachings and practices in imitation of the government's pluralism. Neither Patrick nor the Irish monks ever compromised their faith or church life in imitation of the pagan culture. Instead, the Irish pagans were converted. As a consequence of becoming Christian, hierarchical distinctions receded and slavery ceased.

A third accommodation was made in allowing the church organizational structure to be modified. This was done not because the traditional structures were unimportant, but rather because the essential life and ministries of the church had to be carried out in a different way in order for it to become more easily accepted and established into Irish life. No doubt, this culture challenged Patrick to think deeply about what was essential to the church he was building as distinct from that which was good, but unhelpful for this mission. As we have seen, the Irish monks of the seventh century faced this challenge differently after the Council of Whitby. Today, virtually every denomination and communion in the West is wrestling with this matter, as illustrated by such questions as: Should the church be disestablished? Should we allow non-baptized persons to receive Communion? Should we forsake denominations in favor of independent congregations? One of my great disappointments in church life has been to encounter church members or clergy who are willing to alter the faith of the church in order to preserve their structures, rather than be open to structural change in the name of the changeless faith and the mission of the church. In this, as in many other matters, the work done by Patrick and his successors in Ireland offer much from which we can learn.

As a final word, I will quote another ancient Christian text. This passage predates the writings of Patrick by some 400 years, and is itself a quote from the first Evangelist, in whom, as in no other in quite the same way, the messenger and the message were one. It is attributed to Him by one of his companions, who heard Him pray these words in the presence of him and a few others, but, as he reflected later in compiling an account of these days, he saw that they were intended to be heard by all who would follow Him:

> *"Sanctify them in the truth; thy word is truth. As thou didst send me into the world, so I have sent them into the world. And for their sake I consecrate myself, that they also may be consecrated in truth. I do not pray for these only, but also for those who believe in me through their word, that they may all be one; even as thou, Father, art in me, and I in thee, that they also may be in us, so that the world may believe that thou hast sent me."[111]*

---

[111] John 17:17-21 RSV

Bibliography

1. <u>A History of the Irish Church 400-700 AD</u>: John A. Walsh & Thomas Bradley, c. 1991, The Columba Press, Dublin

2. <u>A Single Ray of the Sun</u>: John Carey, c. 1999, Celtic Studies Publications, North Aberstwyth

3. <u>Art of the Celts</u>: Lloyd & Jennifer Laing, c. 1997, Thames & Hudson Ltd., London

4. <u>Celtic Christianity: Ecology & Holiness</u>: An Anthology by Christopher Bamford and William Parker Marsh, c. 1987, Lindisfarne Press, Hudson, NY

5. <u>Celtic Monasticism</u>: Kathleen Hughes & Ann Hamlin, 1981, Seabury Press, New York, NY

6. <u>Celtic Spirituality:</u> Translated and introduced by Oliver Davies, c. 1999, Paulist Press, Mahwah, NJ

7. <u>Celtic Theology: Humanity, World & God in Early Irish Writing</u>: Thomas O'Loughlin, c. 2000, Continuum, London

8. <u>Early Christian Ireland</u>: Kathleen Hughes, 1972, Cornell University Press, Ithaca, NY

9. <u>Early Christian Ireland:</u> Maire B. & Liam De Paor, c. 1964, Thames & Hudson Ltd., London

10. <u>Irish Art in the Early Christian Period (to 800 AD)</u>: Francoise Hardy, c. 1965, Cornell University Press, Ithaca, NY

11. <u>Irish Spirituality</u>: ed. Michael Maher, c. 1981, Veritas Press, Dublin

12. <u>Journey on the Edges</u>: Thomas O'Loughlin, 2000, Orbis Books, Maryknoll, NY

13. <u>King of Mysteries: Early Irish Religious Writings</u>: John Carey, 2000, Four Courts Press, Dublin

14. <u>Patrick in His Own Words</u>: Joseph Duffy, c. 2000, Veritas Press, Dublin

15. <u>Patrick: The Pilgrim Apostle of Ireland</u>: Maire B. De Paor, c. 1998, Veritas Press, Dublin

16. <u>St. Patrick: His Origins and Career</u>: R.P.C. Hanson, c. 1968, Oxford University Press, Inc., New York, NY

17. <u>St. Patrick: The Man and His Works</u>: Thomas O'Loughlin, c. 1999, Thames & Hudson Ltd., London

18. <u>St. Patrick's World</u>: Liam De Paor, c. 1993, Four Courts Press, Dublin and University of Notre Dame Press, London

19. <u>Saints and Scholars</u>: John Carey, Maire Herbert & Padraig O'Riain, editors, 2001, Four Courts Press, Dublin

20. <u>Spirituality of St. Patrick</u>; Lesley Whiteside, c. 1996, Columba Press, Dublin

21. <u>The Archdiocese of Armagh: A History</u>: Msr. Raymond Murray, c. 2000, Editions Du Signe, Strasbourg, France

22. <u>The Book of Kells</u>: Bernard Meehan, c. 1994, Thames & Hudson Ltd., London

23. <u>The Celtic Way of Evangelism</u>: George Winter III, c. 2000, Abingdon Press, Nashville, TN

24. The Church In Early Irish Society: Kathleen Hughes, c. 1966, London

25. *"The Integral Irish Tradition"*: Pamphlet by Domchady O'Florian, 1968, An Reált, Ireland

26. Understanding the Universe in 7th Century Ireland: Marina Smyth, c. 1996, Boydell Press Woodbridge, Suffolk U.K.

10723629R0

Made in the USA
Lexington, KY
15 August 2011